SOCIAL SCIENCE

C000000635

WELCOME TO CAMBRIDGE SOCIAL SCIENCE

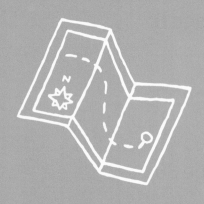

Course objectives

- The *Cambridge Social Science* course has been designed specifically to follow the **LOMCE**. It takes learners on a journey as they discover the wonders of geography and history. Pupils are introduced to topics at a manageable pace, so they can engage with, enjoy and fully assimilate the new concepts.

- Pupils learn about and cement their understanding of new concepts through **projects**. There is an *Explore* project that runs through each unit, in which pupils review and expand upon the concepts presented in the unit. Each individual stage of the *Explore* project feeds into the project finale, in which pupils present or produce something to demonstrate their understanding of the topic.

- Pupils also engage with Social Science in a **hands-on** way by conducting **experiments**. This practises **critical-thinking skills** and collaborative learning.

- Pupils learn about new concepts through discovery. In *Cambridge Social Science*, **learner autonomy** is encouraged through the inclusion of interesting facts and thought-provoking questions. Our aim is for pupils to be inspired by the fun and wondrous world of Social Science.

- **Collaborative learning** is also encouraged through the *Explore* projects, which pupils carry out in pairs, in groups and as a class.

- The course provides pupils with the **linguistic support** that they require

to study Social Science in a second language. The course helps pupils develop their speaking, listening, reading and writing skills. The unit projects give pupils practice of a range of skills and sub-skills.

- Pupils are also given the opportunity to **review the grammar structures** that are presented in *Cambridge Life Adventures*. There are links between the two courses that allow pupils to review Science content in English class and grammar structures in Science class.

- *Cambridge Social Science* is further linked to *Cambridge Life Adventures* in that it provides pupils with practice of the **Cambridge English Qualifications for young learners**. Level 6 provides practice of *B1 Preliminary for Schools* question types.

- **Mixed-ability assessment** provides teachers with support for pupils of different levels within the same class. They focus on lower- and higher-order thinking skills, as well as critical thinking.

- *Cambridge Social Science* has been developed around the **key competences** stipulated in the LOMCE. The course aims to help pupils develop the following key competences: linguistic competence; mathematical competence and basic competences in science and technology; digital competence; learning to learn; social and civic competencies; initiative and entrepreneurship; and cultural awareness and expression.

Course components

Pupil's Book: each unit includes a project, experiments, mixed-ability assessment and practice of the Cambridge English Qualifications for young learners.

Activity Book: each unit includes activities to consolidate and expand upon the concepts introduced in the Pupil's Book, practice of the Cambridge English Qualifications for young learners and a bilingual glossary.

Class audio: provided through the *Digital Lab*, as well as being available to download online at www.thecambridgeteacher.es.

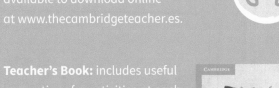

Teacher's Book: includes useful suggestions for activities at each stage of the lesson, answer keys, audio scripts and track numbers for the audio.

Test Generator: allows teachers to build their own tests for each unit, term and end of year assessment.

Digital Lab: includes an interactive digital version of the Pupil's Book with a variety of features to help pupils cement their understanding of key concepts:

- flashcards in digital format
- answer keys
- audio with scripts available
- documentary videos for each unit to engage the pupils in a visual way and allow them to see Social Science in action!

Digital Resource Bank: includes mixed-ability tests, project evaluation grids and curriculum evaluation grids. They are available online at www.thecambridgeteacher.es.

Classroom materials: include posters and a full bank of flashcards to be used across levels. The posters consolidate learning by helping pupils engage with Social Science vocabulary and concepts in the classroom.

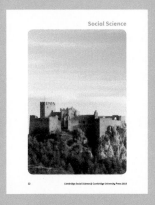

Objective

Pupils will explore how they can use social science in their lives by learning about exciting careers that use elements of the subject. They will think about possible careers for themselves according to their interests.

Key vocabulary

build, discover, create, design, job, plan, investigate, research

Warm up

- With books closed, give pupils two minutes to write down as many jobs as they can. Ask pupils to circle the jobs that they think use social science.

- Draw two columns on the board labelled: *What do we study in social science?* and *What we do in social science class?* Have pupils look quickly through the book and find three ideas for each column. Elicit answers such as: *geography, history, government, law, research, build models, make maps, debate, present,* etc.

Main concepts

- Looking at the careers shown in the lesson and the areas and skills on the board, have pupils look at the list of jobs they wrote to begin the class. Are there any that they didn't think used social science but now do? Discuss as a class.

See examples on the page.

WHERE WILL SOCIAL SCIENCE TAKE ME?

Social science is all around us. You will be surprised at just how many jobs depend on it. It will help you find exciting opportunities to build, discover and shape our world in the future.

What do the jobs in each group have in common?

1 Land surveyor

Geologist

Cartographer

Creates maps using photos taken from planes or space and measurements from the ground using special equipment. You could even map out another planet like Mars!

2 Hydrologist

Environmental planner

Urban planner

Works with communities to design a city that best uses space and resources. They plan where to put parks, homes and the layout of streets to name just a few. Have you got ideas that would improve your community?

3 Teacher

Historian

Journalist

Investigates and reports important news to the public. They must research information, interview people and even go undercover to get the truth to the public. Have you got a story to tell?

Pupils own answers.

Examples:

1 They work outdoors, are active and have opportunities to travel.

2 They work outdoors, plan and design and help people and the environment.

3 They use public speaking, research and work with people.

4

Sociologist

Archaeologist

Anthropologist

Studies how humans develop, live and behave, both in the past and nowadays. Have you ever wondered why football is so popular? An anthropologist could find out!

6

Website designer

Fashion designer

Graphic designer

Combines computers and art with an understanding of society and communications. They design all sorts of images to produce various effects. From the logo of your favourite brand to a sign warning you of danger, the colours, letters and symbols have been carefully chosen.

> In these jobs you can work outdoors / travel / help …

> The jobs in this group require public speaking / computer skills / maths …

5

Judge

Lawyer

Politician

Works in a political system to help a government function. They need different skills and knowledge of law and history, plus the ambition to improve life for people around them.

How does each group of jobs use social science?

🎧 Listen to pupils talk about different jobs. Which photos are they describing?

5

4 They work in a laboratory and outdoors, study people and history and make discoveries.

5 They help people, use law and make speeches.

6 They work with computers, use art and design skills and work with colours and symbols.

B1 Preliminary for Schools
Listening Part 1.

1 Photo 4

2 Photo 2

3 Photo 5

- In groups, pupils choose five careers from the board and write three pros and three cons for each. Pupils should think about the type of work, it's location, etc.

Learn more

- Explain to pupils that surveys are a common aid in finding a career. Using everything they have learned about social science careers, have pupils create a survey to help choose a career. Listen again to the listening activity for ideas. In groups, pupils write questions about likes, abilities and preferences. *Do you like to be outside? Do you prefer group work or working alone? Are you organised? Are you interested in history? Is helping others important?* Finally, pupils carry out the survey and choose which career would suit them best.

Tip

Introduce concepts over two or three lessons. Use the time to establish proper behaviour and structure of pair and group work. The survey is a great way to get to know more about your pupils and find out what interests and excites them.

Track 01
Page 4, *Where will social science take me?*

Track 02
Page 5, *Where will social science take me?* Listening activity

GEOGRAPHY OF SPAIN

Learning objectives

By the end of this unit, pupils will have achieved a greater understanding of the following concepts:

- the geographical boundaries of Spain
- names and locations of the autonomous communities and cities and their capitals
- names and locations of the main rivers of Spain, their sources, mouths, and tributaries
- names and locations of the main mountains and mountain chains of Spain

Competences

This unit covers the following competences:

- Linguistic competence
- Mathematical and basic competences in science and technology
- Digital competence
- Learning to learn
- Cultural awareness and expression

Key vocabulary

Geography: archipelagos, autonomous cites, autonomous communities, border, capital, cave, continent, country, discharge, elevation, flow, glaciers, high, islet, low, mainland, mountain range, mountains, mouth, peak, plateau, relief map, river, source, steep, stream, topographic map, tributaries

Outdoor activities: explore, kayak, nature, ski, surf

Other: beyond, contain, dough, go through, model, mix, run along, split

Cambridge English Qualifications practice

You will find **B1 Preliminary for Schools** activity types in the following exercises:
Pupil's Book, page 10, Listening Part 3
Pupil's Book, page 16, Activity 1 – Writing Part 1
Activity Book, page 5, Activity 7– Reading Part 4
Activity Book, page 6, Activity 9 – Reading Part 1

Throughout this unit, you will find the following **B1 Preliminary for Schools** vocabulary:
along, beyond, border, capital, cave, consist, contain, continent, convince, country, dangerous, exception, explore, famous, flow, high, low, mountain, mention, model, nature, outdoor, peak, permanent, range, recognise, river, ski, steep, stream, surf, surround, useful

Materials needed for *Find out more*

- cardboard
- large bowl
- cup
- flour
- salt
- water
- spoon
- paints
- stickers

Materials needed for other activities

- blank card
- index cards
- examples of postcards, tourism maps and pamphlets
- poster board
- a long pole
- art materials for posters

Explore

The *Explore* project encourages pupils to research the autonomous communities of Spain and their natural features. The pupils will create an exposition showcasing the natural features of a specific community to attract tourism.

The different *Explore* stages focus on the following skills:

- researching and condensing important information
- mapping and directions
- using descriptive language
- giving a presentation
- displaying information and material in an interesting manner

Digital Lab 6 Social Science

Interactive activities

Flashcards

Song: *Autonomous communities*

Video documentary: *Adventuring outdoors*

Objective

Pupils will think about the physical features of Spain that they have seen or experienced firsthand.

Key vocabulary

cave, explore, kayak, mountain, nature, outdoor activities, river, ski, surf

Warm up

- Have one pupil at a time mime an outdoor activity and the class guess. Use activities such as: *hiking, skiing, rock climbing, bird watching, surfing, mountain biking* etc. When the correct answer is said, write it on the board with a cloud drawn around it.

Main concepts

- In groups, pupils discuss locations they know in Spain where each activity on the board and in the book could be done. Have each group write their ideas inside the clouds on the board.

- Play *Have you ever ... ?* Bingo. Pupils draw a 5x5 bingo board. Inside each square they write the name of a place in Spain or an outdoor activity. Pupils walk around and ask: *Have you ever ... ?* If the pupil responds with a *yes*, they can write their name in that square. When a pupil has a line of five different pupils in a row, they can call *Bingo!*

1 Teide; 2 San Sebastián; 3 Sierra Nevada; 4 Ebro Delta; 5 Cueva de Nerja; 6 Guadalquivir River

- Have pupils write a short presentation convincing the class to try an activity they have done or visit somewhere they have been. Encourage pupils to use words such as: *exciting, amazing, life-changing*.

Song
This song focuses on the autonomous communities of Spain.
It can be used on pages 8–9.

Documentary
This documentary focuses on outdoor recreation activities and the places in Spain where they can be done. It can be used to begin the unit to create more interest in the content.

Tip

Watch videos of outdoor activities in Spain to get pupils excited and give them ideas. Share your own stories about any activity or physical feature you've experienced.

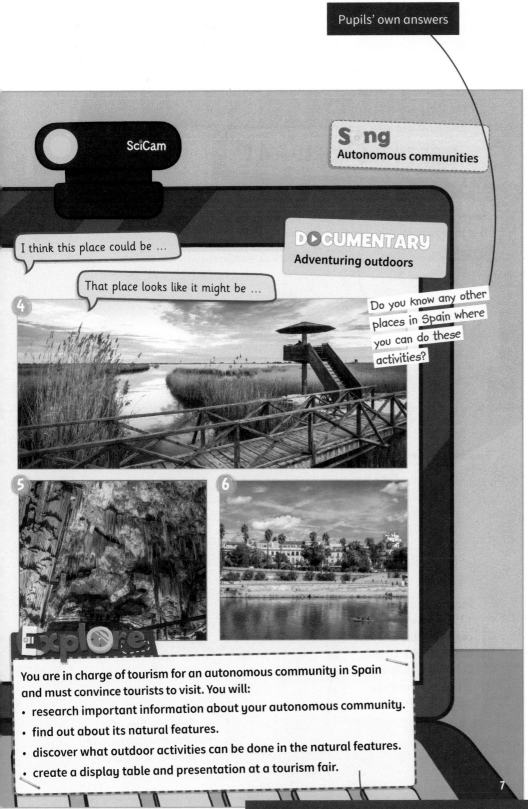

Pupils' own answers

S●ng
Autonomous communities

D▶CUMENTARY
Adventuring outdoors

I think this place could be …

That place looks like it might be …

Do you know any other places in Spain where you can do these activities?

Explore

You are in charge of tourism for an autonomous community in Spain and must convince tourists to visit. You will:

- research important information about your autonomous community.
- find out about its natural features.
- discover what outdoor activities can be done in the natural features.
- create a display table and presentation at a tourism fair.

7

For next lesson … blank card or paper, one pole to attach signs to (optional), postcards, tourist maps, tourist information pamphlets

Group pupils in twos or threes to cover as many of the communities as possible. If there are multiple 6th grade classes, spread the communities over all the classes and plan to have the tourism fair together. Explain that tourism fairs are held to attract visitors and interest. They show off the unique and exciting elements of an area and give examples of things to do and see. Show them examples of tourism websites, pamphlets and posters.

Objective

Pupils will be able to identify the borders of Spain, name the autonomous communities and their capitals and locate them on a map.

Key vocabulary

autonomous cites, autonomous communities, border, capital, continent, country, mainland

Warm up

- With books closed, ask pupils to quickly draw the outline of Spain and label the bodies of water and countries that border it. Have pupils compare with a partner and then look in the book to check.

Main concepts

- Mark the northern wall of the classroom. Have pupils imagine that the walls represent the borders of Spain and decide what each would be, e.g., the northern wall is France, Andorra and the Mar Cantábrico. Pupils create signs and label the walls accordingly.

- Tell pupils to imagine that the classroom is a map of Spain and set the centre of the classroom as Madrid. Using the map and the borders created in the previous activities, pupils work out in which autonomous community their desk is located.

In the southwest of Europe on the Iberian Peninsula.

Five: France, Andorra, Portugal, Morocco and the UK (Gibraltar)

WHERE IN THE WORLD AM I?

Discover... what surrounds Spain and what's in it.

Spain is located in the southwest of Europe on the Iberian Peninsula. It is the fourth largest country on the continent.

ATLANTIC OCEAN

PORTUGAL

Santi Comp

GA

In the west, the border is shared with Portugal and the Atlantic Ocean.

It consists of the Spanish mainland, two autonomous cities in Africa, the Islas Baleares in the Mediterranean Sea and the Islas Canarias in the Atlantic Ocean.

How many countries does Spain share a border with?

Spain is divided into 17 **autonomous communities** and two **autonomous cities**. Each community has got its own borders, capital and flag.

ISLAS CANARIAS

Santa Cruz de Tenerife

Las Palmas de Gran Canaria

Find the flag of an autonomous community hidden in the unit!

The flag of the Comunidad de Madrid on page 13.

8

Learn more

- Make *Where am I?* riddles. Pupils write three or four sentence riddles describing the location of autonomous communities and capital cities and read them to their classmates for them to guess. Provide them with an example such as: *I am in an autonomous community that shares a border with another country and three other communities. It is landlocked and to the west of Madrid. Where am I?*

Tip

If pupils still need more practice, they can copy and label the map in their notebooks. You can also encourage pupils to quiz each other by saying the name of an autonomous community while their partner says the capital.

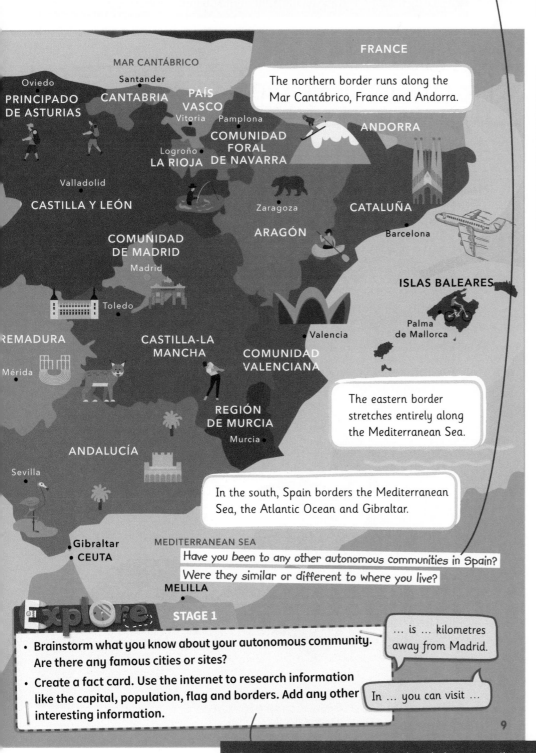

FRANCE

MAR CANTÁBRICO

Oviedo
Santander

PRINCIPADO DE ASTURIAS

CANTABRIA

PAÍS VASCO

Vitoria   Pamplona

ANDORRA

COMUNIDAD FORAL DE NAVARRA

Logroño

LA RIOJA

Valladolid

CASTILLA Y LEÓN

Zaragoza

CATALUÑA

ARAGÓN

Barcelona

COMUNIDAD DE MADRID

Madrid

Toledo

ISLAS BALEARES

REMADURA

Mérida

CASTILLA-LA MANCHA

COMUNIDAD VALENCIANA

Valencia

Palma de Mallorca

REGIÓN DE MURCIA

Murcia

ANDALUCÍA

Sevilla

The northern border runs along the Mar Cantábrico, France and Andorra.

The eastern border stretches entirely along the Mediterranean Sea.

In the south, Spain borders the Mediterranean Sea, the Atlantic Ocean and Gibraltar.

- Gibraltar
- **CEUTA**

MEDITERRANEAN SEA

Have you been to any other autonomous communities in Spain?

Were they similar or different to where you live?

MELILLA

Explore   STAGE 1

- Brainstorm what you know about your autonomous community. Are there any famous cities or sites?
- Create a fact card. Use the internet to research information like the capital, population, flag and borders. Add any other interesting information.

... is ... kilometres away from Madrid.

In ... you can visit ...

9

For next lesson ... index cards, poster board, examples of tourism maps and tourism information pamphlets.

Objective

Pupils will learn the names and locations of the principal mountains and rivers on and around the *Meseta* as well as the tributaries, mouths and sources of the rivers.

Key vocabulary

go through, high, mountains, mouth, plateau, source, split, tributaries

Warm up

- Ask pupils: *What is the Meseta? Where is it located?*

- Have pupils use the map on the previous pages to find which autonomous communities are located on the *Meseta*.

Main concepts

- Draw a large capital letter *D* on the board and tell pupils that it represents the *Meseta*. In pairs, have them discuss where they would place the natural features covered on the page. Then, take volunteers to draw the features on the board. Use different colours to organise the information. Have pupils copy the completed drawing.

Yes!

B1 Preliminary for Schools Listening Part 3

Places: Toledo, Tajo river, Sistema Ibérico, Santander, Cantabría, Picos de Europa, the Meseta, Cordillera Cantábrica, Ria Sella, Mar Cantábrico

Activities: visit museums, hiking, mountain biking, kayaking, surfing

DO I LIVE ON THE MESETA?

Discover... the location and features of the Meseta.

The main natural features of Spain are its many mountains and a large, high **plateau** called the **Meseta Central** in the centre of the country.

Listen to two friends planning a trip. Write down the places and activities they mention.

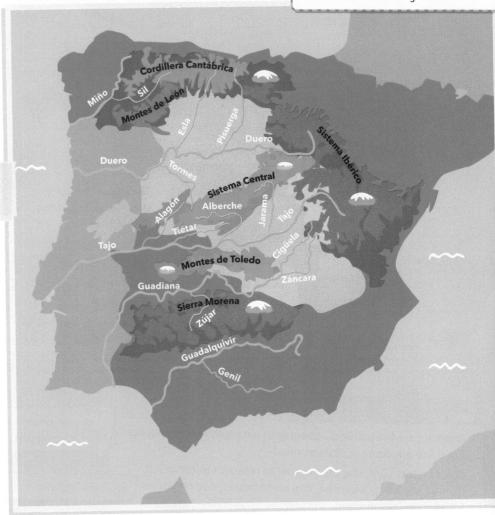

10

The Tajo

On the Meseta

Sistema Central
- Splits the Meseta into north and south
- Goes through two countries

Montes de Toledo
- Smaller group of mountains on the southern part of the Meseta
- Located between the Tajo and Guadiana rivers

River	Source	Mouth	Main tributaries
Duero	Picos de Urbión (Sistema Ibérico)	Porto, Portugal	Pisuerga, Esla, Tormes
Tajo	Sierra de Albarracín (Sistema Ibérico)	Lisbon, Portugal	Jarama, Alberche, Tiétar, Alagón
Guadiana	Castilla-La Mancha	On the border between Spain and Portugal, in Huelva	Cigüela, Záncara, Zújar

Which is the longest river on the Iberian Peninsula?

Around the Meseta

Cordillera Cantábrica
- Borders the northern edge of the Meseta
- Contains the Picos de Europa

Sistema Ibérico
- Borders the eastern edge of the Meseta
- Passes through five communities

Montes de León
- Located between Galicia and the Meseta

Sierra Morena
- Borders the southern edge of the Meseta
- Located between the Guadiana and Guadalquivir rivers

River	Source	Mouth	Main tributaries
Guadalquivir	Cordillera Subbética	Between Huelva and Cádiz	Guadalimar, Guadiana Menor, Jándula, Guadiato, Genil, Viar
Miño	Macizo Galaico	On the border between Spain and Portugal, in Pontevedra	Sil

What are the *source* and the *mouth* of a river?
What is a *tributary*? Look at the map and write definitions.

STAGE 2

- Look at the maps in this unit and find the natural features like mountains and rivers in your community. For any rivers, include the source, tributaries and mouth.
- Draw a map of the community with the rivers and mountains labelled.

11

13

Objective

Pupils will learn the names and locations of the principal mountains and rivers beyond the *Meseta* as well as the tributaries, mouths and sources of the rivers.

Key vocabulary

beyond, contain, discharge, flow, glaciers, low, mountain range, peak, runs along

Warm up

- With books closed, make two columns on the board with the titles; *natural features we have studied* and *natural features we haven't studied yet*. Divide the class into two groups. Pupils from each group must go to the board and write one feature in either column and return to their seat. Then another pupil takes a turn until one team can't think of any more answers.

Main concepts

- Draw a large backwards bubble-letter *C* on the board and tell pupils it represents the area beyond the *Meseta* on the mainland. Elicit the location of the mountains in the *around* category from the previous page and add them to the drawing on the board. Pupils copy the drawing and use the map to add the natural features beyond the *Meseta*.

Everything covered on this page and more!

WHAT LIES BEYOND THE MESETA?

Discover...
more natural features of Spain.

Beyond the Meseta there are five mountain ranges and many rivers.

Macizo Galaico
- Group of low mountains in Galicia

Macizo Galaico · Eo · Navia · Nalón · Sella · Saja · Pas · Nervión · Deva · Bidasoa · Montes Vascos · Ebro · Aragón · Pyrenees · Gállego · Cinca · Segre · Llobregat · Ter · Cordillera Costero-Catalana · Jalón · Turia · Júcar · Mundo · Segura · Sistemas Béticos

Sistemas Béticos
- The Cordillera Penibética runs along the southern coast from Gibraltar to Cabo de Gata. It contains the highest peak on the peninsula (Mulhacén 3,478 metres).
- The Cordillera Subbética is lower and inland, but stretches all the way to Cabo de la Nao in Alicante and beyond to the Islas Baleares. These islands are actually a part of the Cordillera Subbética rising up from the sea floor.

12

Here's the hidden object!

Montes Vascos
- Small group of mountains in the north

Pyrenees
- Form the border between France and Spain
- Contain hundreds of peaks over 2,000 metres high

Cordillera Costero-Catalana
- Runs along the Mediterranean coast between the mouth of the Ebro and the Pyrenees

Are there any glaciers in Spain? Find out more about them.

Rivers that flow into the Mediterranean share similar characteristics. Most of them are short and carry very little water.

The exception is the **Ebro**, the longest river in Spain, which discharges more water than any other river in Spain.

The rivers of the north are short with high levels of water flowing through them to the Mar Cantábrico.

In your notebook, complete the table with the rivers shown on the map.

Tributaries of the Ebro	Rivers that end in the Mediterranean Sea	Rivers that end in the Mar Cantábrico

Can you think of reasons why rivers in the north and south are so different?

Explore · STAGE 3

- Discuss with a partner what outdoor activities you have done. Were they exciting, dangerous, or enjoyable? Where did you do them?
- Research the outdoor activities that can be done in your autonomous community. Write down two you would like to try and where you can try them.

I have … in the …

It was so much fun!

Was it … ?

13

- Complete the drawing on the board as a class to make sure the pupils have correctly placed the natural features.
- Give pupils time to complete the table on the rivers individually and compare answers with classmates.

Learn more

- Play *How do we get to …?* In groups, pupils write in their notebooks how to get to a location from Madrid travelling in a straight line. One group asks, *How do we get to …?*, while the other groups write down the directions. Pupils must say the direction travelled and what natural features they will go over, go through, pass by or cross. For example; *How do we get to Burgos?: go north, go through the Sistema Central, cross the Duero, pass the Sistema Ibérico … etc.*

The climate in the south has much less precipitation and the land is flatter.

Yes. They are in the Pyrenees, but they are melting fast. There were glaciers in the Sierra Nevada and the Picos de Europa but they melted away.

Review some vocabulary pupils can use to describe outdoor activities. Remind them that the experiences don't have to be positive. Help pupils get better search results by recommending they search for videos and travel blogs. Give time for pupils to share what they found with their group and have them choose the best activities to use in their exposition.

For next lesson … card or paper, examples of postcards and tourism posters

Objective

Pupils will learn the about the natural features of the Spanish islands.

Key vocabulary

archipelagos, elevation, islet, steeper, stream, topographic map

Warm up

- With books closed, ask pupils to guess how many islands are in each archipelago. In small groups, pupils see who can name the most islands (Baleares: Mallorca, Ibiza, Formentera, Menorca, Isla de Cabrera; Canarias: Lanzarote, Fuerteventura, Gran Canaria, Santa Cruz de Tenerife, Santa Cruz de la Palma, Gomera, El Hierro).

Main concepts

- After reading through the page, pupils make sentences describing each of the archipelagos. They read them to the class and pupils shout out which is *Canarias*, *Baleares* or *both*.

Learn more

- Play *20 questions*. Pupils use the maps in the unit and choose a mountain, river, or capital. Other pupils ask *Yes* or *No* questions to find out what they are. For example; *Are you a … ? Are you on/ beyond … ? Are you north of … ? Are you between … and … ?*

The Cordillera Subbética

Extra Activity, page 90:
Pupils create a topographic map of a mountain they made with plasticine.

Spain's archipelagos

Advise pupils to start where the gradient is less and move around the island to find the least steep parts.

WHAT'S GOING ON OFF THE PENINSULA?

Discover... the archipelagos of Spain.

Beyond the Meseta, and away from the peninsula, lie Spain's two **archipelagos**: the Islas Baleares and the Islas Canarias.

- Five main islands
- Only has one low mountain range
- Mainly flat with a few hilly areas

- No permanent rivers, but short streams that flow only when it rains
- Contain a few small islets

Look back
Which mountain range are these islands formed from?

Islas Baleares

- Seven main islands
- Located about 150 kilometres off the coast of North Africa
- Contain Spain's highest peak: Mount Teide at 3,718 metres
- Volcanic islands formed by lava seeping out from the Earth's crust on the ocean floor

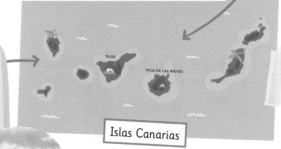

Islas Canarias

A **topographic map** shows changes of elevation. The closer the lines are together, the steeper the area.

Use the map to plan out how you would climb Mount Teide.

Explore STAGE 4

- The Islas Canarias are home to the tallest mountain in Spain and this is used to attract visitors. Find something in your autonomous community that can be written as a superlative.
- Make a postcard featuring it to use in your tourism display.

14

Show examples of postcards and tourism posters to help pupils plan out their designs. They can research information at home and create the postcards as a group in the next lesson. Help pupils find better search results by recommending they search the official tourism websites.

For next lesson … cardboard, large bowl, cup, flour, salt, water, spoon, paints, stickers

Planning a hike, deciding where to build roads, bridges or towns, planning for natural disasters like floods or fire and much more.

By making a relief map.

HOW CAN WE SHOW SPAIN IN 3-D?

Background: Relief maps show the changes in elevations like a topographic map, but in three dimensions. They are useful when studying rivers and mountains.

Materials: cardboard, large bowl, cup, flour, salt, water, spoon, paints, stickers

Task: In groups make a large relief map of Spain.

Step 1: Draw an outline of Spain on the cardboard. Add in basic outlines of the mountain ranges.

Step 2: Make the dough. Mix two cups of flour with one cup of salt in the large bowl. Slowly add one cup of water and mix. If it is too sticky, add more flour.

Step 3: Place the dough on the map. Start with the mountain ranges, then fill in the rest of Spain.

Step 4: Paint with different colours for the different elevations.

Step 5: Write labels for the mountains and rivers and stick them to the map when it is dry. Create a key for the colours of the map.

Find Out more...

Discover... how to make a relief map of Spain.

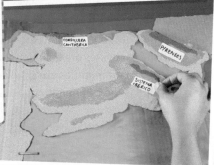

What do we use relief maps for?

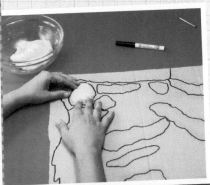

15

Objective

Pupils will learn to follow instructions and make a 3-D model using flour, salt and water.

Key vocabulary

cardboard, dough, mix, model, relief map

Warm up

• In the centre of the board write, *Productive and fantastic Find out More.* Ask pupils to think of what should be done to keep the project on task and make a mind map. Elicit answers such as stay organised, work as a team, keep areas clean, ask questions when unsure.

Main concept

• Put pupils in groups of four or five. Remind them to put the water in a few parts at a time until it no longer sticks to their hands.

• When maps are dry, pupils paint and label with stickers. If short on time, the maps can be painted while still wet.

Learn more

• In groups, pupils experiment with the finished maps by closing their eyes, feeling the map and trying to find the places their classmates shout out.

Language Review answers

1 Example answer: Hi Nick, Thanks for your email. It's great that you got Spain for your project. If I were you, I'd focus on the Comunidad de Madrid. I live there so I know lots about it! Of course we can video chat. How about tomorrow after school at 6 pm? Bye for now.

> This activity gives pupils practice of *B1 Preliminary for Schools*, Writing Part 1

2 b The Islas Canarias don't contain any permanent rivers. Nor do the Islas Baleares.

c The Duero flows into the Atlantic Ocean. So does the Tajo.

d The Comunidad Valenciana is made up of three provinces. So is Aragón.

e Extremadura hasn't got a coastline. Nor has La Rioja.

f The Montes de Toledo are located on the Meseta. So is the Sistema Central.

3 a I am good at … *pupils' own answer*

b I am afraid of … *pupils' own answer*

c I am keen on visiting … *pupils' own answer*

d It is famous for … *pupils' own answer*

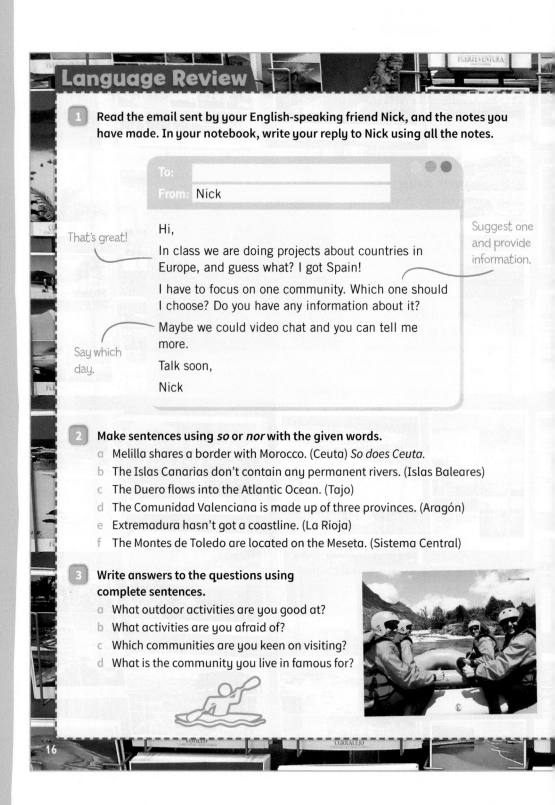

Language Review

1 Read the email sent by your English-speaking friend Nick, and the notes you have made. In your notebook, write your reply to Nick using all the notes.

To:
From: Nick

That's great!

Hi,

In class we are doing projects about countries in Europe, and guess what? I got Spain!

Suggest one and provide information.

I have to focus on one community. Which one should I choose? Do you have any information about it?

Say which day.

Maybe we could video chat and you can tell me more.

Talk soon,

Nick

2 Make sentences using *so* or *nor* with the given words.
a Melilla shares a border with Morocco. (Ceuta) *So does Ceuta.*
b The Islas Canarias don't contain any permanent rivers. (Islas Baleares)
c The Duero flows into the Atlantic Ocean. (Tajo)
d The Comunidad Valenciana is made up of three provinces. (Aragón)
e Extremadura hasn't got a coastline. (La Rioja)
f The Montes de Toledo are located on the Meseta. (Sistema Central)

3 Write answers to the questions using complete sentences.
a What outdoor activities are you good at?
b What activities are you afraid of?
c Which communities are you keen on visiting?
d What is the community you live in famous for?

16

Encourage pupils to revise the unit content using the techniques from page 79.

Content Review

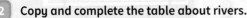

Assessment link

For more Unit 1 activities go to page 78

1 Choose the odd one out and say why.

a Sistema Central / Montes de Toledo / Montes de León
The Sistema Central and the Montes de Toledo are on the Meseta, but the Montes de León are around it.

b Cordillera Penibética / Picos de Europa / Cordillera Subbética

c Ebro / Júcar / Duero

d Cuenca / León / Burgos

e Región de Murcia / Cantabria / Andalucía

2 Copy and complete the table about rivers.

River	Source	Mouth	Tributaries	Communities passed through
Ebro				
Tajo				
Duero				
Guadiana				
Guadalquivir				

Explore   FINALE

- In your group, decide what will attract tourists to your autonomous community. Use the information you have gathered, as well as including cultural elements like festivals and food.

- Make a display highlighting the best parts of your community with posters, 3-D models, pictures and even items from the area. Plan how to arrange them on a table.

- Finally, write out what to say when people visit your display. The more enthusiastic you are, the more excited people will be to visit your community!

17

Find a time and a place to hold the tourism fair that allows other classes and teachers to visit. Inform the pupils that the visitors to their booths will vote on their favourite. Show the pupils the space they will have to create a booth. Provide some vocabulary help and examples to improve the pupils' presentations. Give them time to create their displays and remind them to practise their presentations a number of times.

Content Review answers

1 b The Picos de Europa are in the Cordillera Cantábrica but the others are in the Sistemas Béticos.

c The Duero ends in the Atlantic Ocean but the others flow into the Mediterranean Sea.

d Cuenca is in Castilla-La Mancha, but the others are in Castilla y León.

e Cantabria's coast is on the Mar Cantábrico, but the others have coasts on the Mediterranean Sea.

2 Ebro: Source - Cordillera Cantábrica; Mouth - Deltebre; Cataluña; Tributaries - Segre; Jalón; Gallego; Aragón; Communities - Cantabria; Castilla y León; La Rioja; Aragón; Navarra; Cataluña

Tajo: Source - Sierra de Albarracín (Sistema Ibérico); Mouth - Lisbon; Portugal; Tributaries - Jarama; Alberche; Tiétar; Alagón; Communities - Castilla-La Mancha; Comunidad de Madrid; Extremadura

Duero: Source - Picos de Urbión (Sistema Ibérico); Mouth - Porto; Portugal; Tributaries - Pisuerga; Esla; Tormes; Communities - Castilla y León

Guadiana: Source - Castilla-La Mancha; Mouth - on the border between Spain and Portugal, Huelva; Tributaries - Cigüela; Záncara; Zújar; Communities - Castilla-La Mancha; Extremadura

Guadalquivir: Source - Cordillera Subbética; Mouth - between Huelva and Cádiz; Tributaries - Genil; Guadiana Menor; Communities - Andalucía

Think about it answers

1 Mar Cantábrico, France, Andorra, Mediterranean Sea, Morocco, Gibraltar, Atlantic Ocean, Portugal

2 Nine: Galicia, Santiago de Compostela; Asturias, Oviedo; Cantabría, Santander; La Rioja, Logroño; País Vasco, Vitoria; Aragón, Zaragoza; Comunidad de Madrid, Madrid; Castilla-La Mancha, Toledo; Extremadura, Mérida

3 Andalucía, Cataluña, Ceuta, Melilla, Región de Murcia, Comunidad Valenciana, Islas Baleares

4 Duero, Tajo, Miño, Guadiana, Guadalquivir

5 Example answers: It goes through Spain and Portugal. It splits the Meseta into two regions, north and south. It is between the Duero and the Tajo rivers.

6 Sierra Morena, Sistema Ibérico, Cordillera Cantábrica, Montes de León

7 The Mulhacén is located in the Cordillera Penibético.

8 The Pyrenees form the border between France, Andorra and Spain. The rivers Miño and Guadiana form parts of the border with Portugal.

9 Ebro, Nalón, Sella

10 Example answers: There aren't any permanent rivers on either archipelago. They both form their own autonomous communities. The Islas Canarias are in the Atlantic Ocean and the Islas Baleares are in the Mediterranean Sea. The Islas Canarias are volcanic islands and the Islas Baleares are not.

Think harder answers

1 Example answers: La Molina, Pyrenees; Baqueira-Beret, Pyrenees, Navacerrada, Sistema Central, Sierra Nevada, Sistemas Béticos

2 Pupils' own answers

3 Example answer: The many mountain ranges of Spain made travel difficult to many areas, so these areas developed unique traditions and cultures.

4 It is different because its source is in the north of Spain where the climate has more precipitation and it has many tributaries flowing into it.

5 Pupils' own answers

6 The Sierra Nevada and the Picos de Europa.

7 Starting in Cataluña and driving through País Vasco.

8 Madrid, Barcelona, Valencia, Sevilla, Zaragoza

9 Pupils' own answers

10 Pupils' own answers

UNIT 1 TRACKLIST

GEOGRAPHY OF EUROPE

Learning objectives

By the end of this unit, pupils will have achieved a greater understanding of the following concepts:

- the geographical limits of Europe
- the location and names of the countries of Europe and their capitals
- the location and names of the main mountain ranges and rivers of Europe

Competences

This unit covers the following competences:

- Linguistic competence
- Mathematical and basic competences in science and technology
- Digital competence
- Learning to learn
- Cultural awareness and expression
- Initiative and entrepreneurship

Key vocabulary

Oceans and seas: Arctic Ocean, Atlantic Ocean, Black Sea, Caspian Sea, Mediterranean Sea

Rivers: Danube, Dnieper, Don, drain into, Ebro, Elbe, Loire, Oder, Pechora, Po, Rhine, Rhône, Seine, Tajo, Ural, Volga, watershed

Mountains: Alps, Balkan Mountains, Carpathian Mountains, Caucasus Mountains, Pyrenees, Ural Mountains

Bridges: arch bridge, bridge, Romans, shape, spread out, weight

Other: Asia, border, civilisations, culture, Europe, geography, hemisphere, natural features, navigable, peninsula, success

Cambridge English Qualifications practice

You will find *B1 Preliminary for Schools* activity types in the following exercises:
Pupil's Book, Page 20 – Listening Part 3
Pupil's Book, Page 26, Activity 2 – Reading Part 3
Activity Book, Page 13, Activity 11 – Reading Part 2

Throughout this unit, you will find the following *B1 Preliminary for Schools* vocabulary: active, attraction, border, bridge, central, culture, despite, drier, due to, enormous, Europe, evenly, except, expedition, flat, freeze, geography, persuade, provide, report, shape, southeast, tourist, weight, well-known

Materials needed for *Find out more*

- paper
- ruler
- pencil
- lollipop sticks
- wood glue

Materials needed for other activities

- A4 card or paper
- spool of string or ribbon
- scissors
- blank political maps of Europe

Explore

The *Explore* project encourages pupils to research and explore the cites and natural features of Europe. They will plan an end-of-year class trip and present their idea to the class. The different *Explore* stages focus on the following skills:

- conducting a survey of their classmates
- researching online
- planning out time
- reading maps and planning routes
- creating a slide presentation

Digital Lab 6 Social Science

Interactive activities

Flashcards

Song: *Cruising the continent*

Video documentary: *Bridges and tunnels*

Objective

Pupils will think about the relationship between cities and the natural features around them and talk about their experiences in other European countries.

Key vocabulary

civilisations, culture, geography, natural features, success

Warm up

• In small groups, pupils take turns to mime outdoor activities while the rest of the group guesses what they are doing and where they are. For example; *You are hiking in the mountains. You are kayaking down a river.*

Main concepts

• Play *Two truths and one lie*. Have pupils write three sentences about any country in Europe. They can be about places they have or haven't visited, or facts they know or have made up about a country or city. Two sentences should be true and one a lie. Pupils then read their sentences aloud to a partner who must guess which one is a lie. Have them change partners and play again.

• In pairs, pupils think of three advantages and three disadvantages to having a river run through a city. Have pupils share with the class and debate.

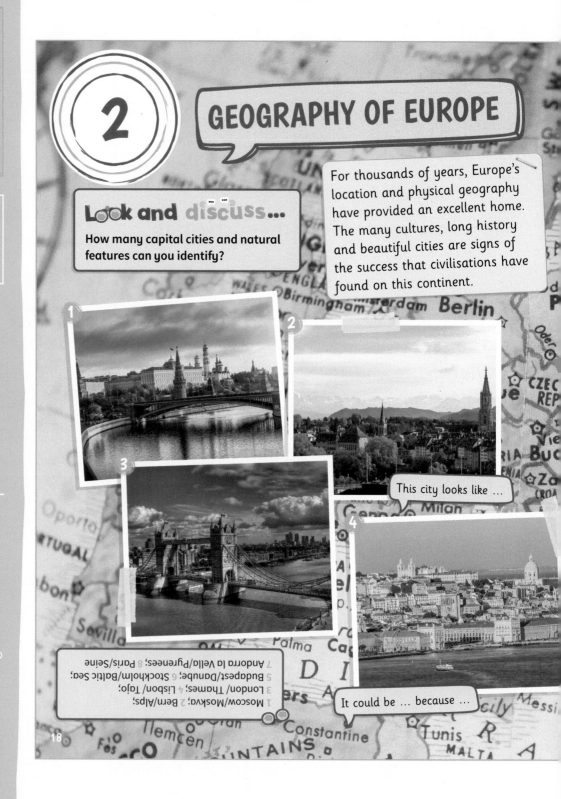

2 **GEOGRAPHY OF EUROPE**

L👓k and discuss...

How many capital cities and natural features can you identify?

For thousands of years, Europe's location and physical geography have provided an excellent home. The many cultures, long history and beautiful cities are signs of the success that civilisations have found on this continent.

This city looks like …

It could be … because …

1 Moscow/Moskva; 2 Bern/Alps;
3 London/ Thames; 4 Lisbon/ Tajo;
5 Budapest/Danube; 6 Stockholm/Baltic Sea;
7 Andorra la Vella/Pyrenees; 8 Paris/Seine

18

Yes. In the past, rivers provided transport and defence, but they can create problems such as how to connect both sides of a river and flooding. Mountains made it difficult to travel to and from the city, but they also provided protection and resources.

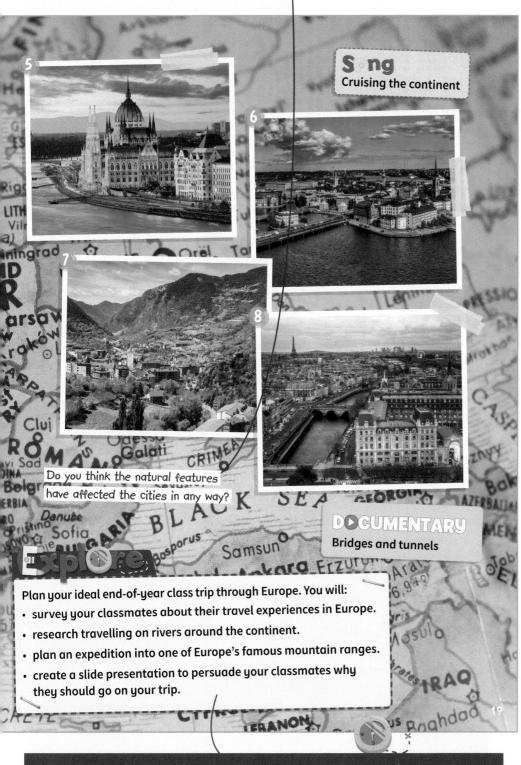

S•ng
Cruising the continent

Do you think the natural features have affected the cities in any way?

D▸CUMENTARY
Bridges and tunnels

Explore

Plan your ideal end-of-year class trip through Europe. You will:

- survey your classmates about their travel experiences in Europe.
- research travelling on rivers around the continent.
- plan an expedition into one of Europe's famous mountain ranges.
- create a slide presentation to persuade your classmates why they should go on your trip.

19

Tell pupils to imagine that they are in charge of an end-of-year trip for the entire class. Discuss past class trips or excursions and elicit elements that school trips should have. Remind pupils to keep their ideas organised in their notebooks for the final stage when they will combine their ideas with others.

Learn more

- Have pupils elaborate on one of their truths from the warm-up activity by writing a short description of their experience. Encourage pupils to use varied vocabulary to create a more interesting story. Have them read their writings to their classmates.

Song

This song focuses on some of the countries of Europe. It can be used on pages 20–21 as a review.

Documentary

The documentary focuses on different bridges and tunnels found around Europe. It can be used on pages 22–24 and on page 25.

Tip

Search for images online of European capital cites like those covered on the page to expand on the lesson. Show the landmarks, sites and natural features associated with the cities.

Objective

Pupils will learn the geographical boundaries of the European continent and the name and location of its countries and their capitals.

Key vocabulary

Arctic Ocean, Asia, Atlantic Ocean, Black Sea, border, Caspian Sea, Caucasus Mountains, Europe, hemisphere, Mediterranean Sea, peninsula, Ural Mountains

Warm up

- Put pupils in pairs with a piece of blank A4 paper and their books. One pupil closes their eyes and draws the European continent while the other dictates looking at the map in their book. Remind pupils of commands such as: *go up, left, down.* Have pupils switch roles every minute until the outline is finished.

Main concepts

- To help pupils remember the large number of countries, divide Europe into smaller sections and create Mnemonic devices. For example: Norway, Sweden, Finland Russia: *No Smelly Food, Rachael.* Switzerland, Germany, Luxembourg, Belgium, Netherlands, Denmark: *Silly George Likes Buying New Donkeys.*

The Ural and Caucasus Mountains

Asia and then Africa

Pupils' own answers

B1 Preliminary for Schools Listening Part 3.
Oslo (Norway), Stockholm (Sweden), Bern (Switzerland), Prague (Czech Republic), Vienna (Austria), Sofia (Bulgaria), Bucharest (Romania), Athens (Greece)

WHERE DOES EUROPE END AND ASIA BEGIN?

Discover... the limits, countries and capitals of the European continent.

The European continent is located in the northern hemisphere. It is the second smallest continent.

Despite Europe's small size, it has the third highest population of all the continents and contains around 50 countries.

What two continents have a higher population than Europe?

Capital cities are usually the place where a government has its offices and operates. They are large cities, but not always the largest in the country.

Are you surprised by any of the capital cities on the map?

Look at the map. Can you find …
… the smallest countries in Europe?
… all the countries that touch more than one body of water?
… the southernmost point?
… all the landlocked countries?
… all the peninsulas?
… all the countries with territory on two continents?
Now think of some more questions and see if your classmates can answer them.

 Listen to the weather report for capital cities in Europe. Write down the cities you hear and match them to their countries.

20

- Vatican City, Andorra, Monaco, Luxembourg, San Marino, Liechtenstein, Malta

- Spain, France, Italy, Russia, Turkey, Norway, United Kingdom, Ireland

- Punta de Tarifa, Spain

- Andorra, Slovakia, Luxembourg, Macedonia, Vatican City, Serbia, Belarus, Austria, Czech Republic, Moldova, Switzerland, Hungary, San Marino, Liechtenstein, Kosovo

- Balkan, Iberian, Italian, Scandinavian

- Spain, Turkey, Russia

ICELAND
Reykjavík

ATLANTIC OCEAN

IRELA

PORTUGAL
Lisbon

Europe is separated from Asia in the east by the **Ural Mountains**. The continent forms an enormous peninsula surrounded by the **Arctic Ocean** to the north, the **Atlantic Ocean** to the west and the **Mediterranean Sea** to the south.

ARCTIC OCEAN

NORWAY
Oslo
Stockholm
SWEDEN
FINLAND
Helsinki
Tallinn
ESTONIA
Riga
LATVIA
RUSSIA
Moscow
NORTH SEA
DENMARK
Copenhagen
BALTIC SEA
LITHUANIA
Vilnius
Minsk
BELARUS
Amsterdam
Berlin
NETHERLANDS
POLAND
Warsaw
URAL MOUNTAINS
Brussels
BELGIUM
GERMANY
Kiev
LUXEMBOURG
Luxembourg
Prague
CZECH REPUBLIC
UKRAINE
Paris
SLOVAKIA
Bratislava
KAZAKHSTAN
Astana
FRANCE
LIECHTENSTEIN
Vaduz
Vienna
AUSTRIA
Budapest
MOLDOVA
Chisinau
Bern
SWITZERLAND
HUNGARY
SLOVENIA
Ljubljana
Zagreb
CROATIA
ROMANIA
CAUCASUS MOUNTAINS
SAN MARINO
San Marino
BOSNIA & HERZEGOVINA
Sarajevo
Belgrade
SERBIA
Bucharest
MONACO
Monaco
ITALY
MONTENEGRO
Podgorica
Pristina
KOSOVO
Sofia
BULGARIA
BLACK SEA
CASPIAN SEA
GEORGIA
Tbilisi
ANDORRA
dorra la Vella
Rome
VATICAN CITY
Tirana
MACEDONIA
Skopje
ALBANIA
Ankara
ARMENIA
Yerevan
AZERBAIJAN
Baku
MEDITERRANEAN SEA
GREECE
TURKEY
Athens
MALTA
Valletta
CYPRUS
Nicosia

The south-east corner is bordered by the **Black Sea**, the **Caucasus Mountains** and the **Caspian Sea**.

Explore — STAGE 1

- Survey your classmates about their travel experiences in Europe. What cities have they visited? What did they like or dislike? Would they go back?
- Using this information, choose two capital cities to begin your trip and research the main tourist attractions in each. Write your ideas in your notebook.

21

In class, help create the surveys by reviewing grammar and vocabulary needed and discuss what information you would need to know to plan a trip for other people. Give pupils time to survey their classmates and remind them to take notes to use later. At home, they research and decide on two cities to visit and record information such as location, language, currency and tourist destinations in their notebooks.

For next lesson ... spool of string or ribbon, blank card or paper for each group, scissors, blank political maps of Europe

- Play *Capital Bingo!* Tell pupils to draw a 5x5 bingo board and write a European country in each square. When they have finished, instruct them to close their books. Call out the names of capital cities. If pupils have that country, they mark the square. Five in a row is *Bingo!*

Learn more

- Listen to the weather report again and tell pupils to make their own weather report with their partner from the Warm-up activity using the map they made. Pupils choose five capitals cites and draw weather symbols where they are located on the map. Tell them to write a short report and practise a few times before performing for the whole class.

Tip

The number of countries and exact boundaries of Europe are different according to different organisations and institutions. Remind pupils the set definition of a country or continent can be debated and be open to other points of view.

Objective

Pupils will be able to name and locate the main rivers of Europe on a map.

Key vocabulary

Danube, Dnieper, Don, drain into, Dvina, Ebro, Elbe, Loire, navigable, Oder, Pechora, Po, Rhine, Rhône, Seine, Tajo, Thames, Tiber, Ural, Volga, watershed

Warm up

- Write the word *navigable* on the board and ask pupils what they think it means. Give them clues until you arrive at the answer: *an area of water that can be travelled on by boat.*

Main concepts

- Put pupils in groups, assign them a river from the map and give them a half sheet of card or paper. Tell them they are going to make an information card for their river with everything they can learn from the page: *source, mouth, places it passes through*, etc. Remind them to make it bright and colourful.

- Write the lengths of the rivers on the board and mention that the courses of rivers are always changing so most lengths aren't exact. Have each group guess which river is theirs. Pupils measure and cut string to represent the length of their river

In the Caspian Sea

WHERE IS THE MOUTH OF THE VOLGA?

Discover... the important rivers in Europe.

Most of Europe's major rivers are long with a steady flow of water, which allows boats to travel along them. There are many important cities on their banks and busy ports at their mouths.

Rivers can be grouped by the body of water that they drain into. The group is called a **watershed**. There are five major watersheds in Europe.

Look back

Which Spanish rivers drain into the Atlantic Ocean?

The Tajo, Duero, Miño, Guadiana and Guadalquivir.

22

Pechora 1,809 km, Ural 2,428 km, Volga 3,530 km, Don 1,950 km, Dnieper 2,290 km, Oder 854 km, Elbe 1094 km, Rhine 1233 km, Rhône 812 km, Po 652 km, Seine 777 km, Loire 1,006 km, Ebro 910 km, Tajo 1,007 km, Danube 2,856 km, Northern Dvina 744 km, Western Dvina 1,020 km, Tiber 406 km, Thames 346 km.

Learn more

- Hand out a blank political map of Europe to each pupil. Tell them that they are going to combine the political and physical maps of Europe. First, they need to add and label the capital cities. Next, instruct pupils to draw in the rivers using the cites as a reference with a bright colour.

Here's the hidden object!

The Ebro, Tiber and Rhône

1 The Atlantic watershed contains many well-known rivers like the Thames passing through London, the Seine winding through Paris, and the Rhine starting up in the Alps and running 1,233 kilometres to the ocean.

2 The Arctic watershed rivers are mainly located in Northern Russia and sometimes freeze in the winter.

3 The rivers of the Mediterranean watershed have a low flow due to being in areas with a drier climate and most are not useful for transport by boat.

Name three rivers that drain into the Mediterranean Sea.

4 Rivers in the southeast are long with high flows. They run through a very flat area and drain into either the Black Sea, like the Danube …

5 … or the Caspian Sea, like the Volga. The Volga and the Danube are the two longest rivers in Europe.

Find out how long these rivers are. Which countries does each river pass through?

Most rivers begin in the mountains. Find out about them on the next page!

Tip

Have pupils arrange their river information cards on a wall in the classroom. They can decide to do it from longest to shortest, east to west or in groups by watershed.

Explore STAGE 2

- Most capital cities are located on rivers that boats can still travel on. Choose a city with a river and use the internet to see if there are any boat cruises or tours you can take.
- Draw out the course of the river, marking the locations you visit along the way.
- Describe your tour to a partner.

The tour starts at …

Next, …

Finally, …

23

This can be done at home or in the computer lab. Pupils use the map in their books to choose cities with rivers and then look them up online. Pupils write their notes in their notebooks. Check their progress by listening to their descriptions during the next lesson.

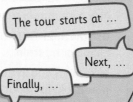

Volga: 3,530 km, Russia;
Danube: 2,856 km; Germany, Austria, Slovakia, Hungary, Croatia, Serbia, Bulgaria, Romania, Moldova, Ukraine

For next lesson … A4 paper or card, blank political maps of Europe from this lesson

Objective

Pupils will be able to name and locate the main mountain ranges of Europe on a map.

Key vocabulary

Alps, Balkan Mountains, Caucasus Mountains, Carpathian Mountains, Pyrenees, Ural Mountains

Warm up

- Tell pupils that the names of some body parts are also names for parts of rivers and mountains. Foot: *base of a mountain*; face: *side of a mountain*; mouth: *where a river drains into a larger body of water*; spine: *a thin ridge of a mountain*

Main concepts

- Put pupils into six groups and assign them each one of the following: *Mulhacén, Mont Blanc, Teide, Elbrus, Matterhorn, Etna.* On a piece of A4 card tell them to make a scaled version of the mountain. (Scale: 1 cm = 200m) and make a poster with its name, height and any other interesting information.

Learn more

- Using their maps of Europe from the previous lesson, pupils add the mountains from page 22.

It's on page 23 in the river

The Alps are in Central Europe.

The Caucasus Mountains are on the southeast border of Europe.

The Carpathian Mountains are in Central Europe, east of the Alps.

The Ural Mountains are in Russia, forming the eastern border of Europe.

The Scandinavian Mountains are on the Scandinavian Peninsula.

HOW HIGH CAN I CLIMB?

Discover... the mountains of Europe.

Large areas of the European continent are flat. Most of the mountains are in the south, except for the Ural Mountains on the eastern border and the Scandinavian Mountains running along the Scandinavian Peninsula.

Look back

Where are these mountain ranges? Use the map on page 22 to find out!

The **Alps** stretch across eight countries, from France to Slovenia.

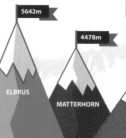

The **Caucasus Mountains** form a border between Europe and Asia, and contain Mount Elbrus, the highest peak in Europe.

Find the peak of the Matterhorn hidden in the unit!

5642m

4808m

4478m

3718m

3329m

MONT BLANC

ELBRUS

MATTERHORN

TEIDE

ETNA

963m

CUATRO TORRES MADRID

The **Carpathian Mountains** are in central Europe. The Danube runs between them and the Balkan Mountains at a place called the Iron Gate.

Mount Etna, on the Italian island of Sicily, is Europe's most active volcano. It is also very tall.

How does it compare with other mountains and volcanoes in Europe?

Explore — STAGE 3

- Pick a mountain range you would like to visit on the class trip.
- Use the internet to find out the best way to see it like skiing, hiking or by train.
- Plan out a day in the mountains. In your notebook, list what you will do and see.

I would love to see / visit ...

24

Have pupils prepare this stage at home. Advise them that hiking, climbing or travel blogs are excellent places to find information on excursions to the mountains.

It is the highest active volcano in Europe outside the Caucasus. It is the highest peak in Italy south of the Alps. Only Mount Teide in Tenerife is bigger than Etna. It is one of the world's most active volcanoes.

For next lesson ... paper, ruler, pencil, lollipop sticks, wood glue

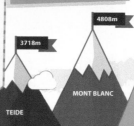

> Using maths and shapes like arches and triangles and strong materials like steel.

HOW DO WE MAKE BRIDGES STRONG?

Find out more...

Discover... different types of bridge design.

Background: Building bridges has been one of the most important tasks in connecting cities and countries. The Romans mastered the arch bridge and built hundreds of them all around Europe. The arch shape evenly spreads the weight down to the bases. They were so strong that many structures are still standing today.

Truss bridges were the first modern bridges. They use triangles instead of arches to spread out weight. The triangles can be grouped together, which makes them lighter and stronger than arched bridges.

Materials: paper, ruler, pencil, lollipop sticks, wood glue

Task: In small groups, make a model of a bridge using the lollipop sticks and wood glue. The bridge should span a distance between two tables and use no more than 100 sticks.

Step 1: Use the information on bridges on this page and draw out a basic plan before starting.

Step 2: Begin building. Be careful and precise. The better built it is, the stronger it will be!

Step 3: Test your bridge by placing weight on it like books. Whose bridge is the strongest?

25

Objective

Pupils will learn about bridge design and history. They will experiment with different building techniques and create their own.

Key vocabulary

arch bridge, bridge, Romans, shape, spread out, truss bridge, weight

Warm up

- Play the documentary again and discuss the bridges seen. Elicit answers to the following questions: *What were they made of? What did they look like? Were some more functional and others more beautiful? Have they seen any mentioned in the video in person?*

Main concepts

- Show pupils the material they have to use to create the bridge and the distance they need to cover, around 30 cm. Discuss what type of bridge would be best and elicit the answer of a truss bridge. Remind pupils to plan out the bridge first to make sure they have enough sticks.

Learn more

- Pupils name and decorate their bridge to be displayed for the rest of the school to see.

Language Review answers

1 b Europe has fewer people than Africa.

c In Paris there are more bridges over the river than in London.

d The south of Europe has more mountains than the north.

e The Volga passes through fewer countries than the Danube.

2 1 b

2 b

3 b

4 c

This activity gives pupils practice of *B1 Preliminary for Schools* Reading Part 3.

Language Review

1 **In your notebook, rewrite the sentences using *more … than / fewer … than*.**

a Spain is a very mountainous country. Estonia is a flat country.
Spain has more mountains than Estonia.

b Europe has the third highest population. Africa has the second highest population.

c In Paris there are 37 bridges over the Seine. In London there are 33 bridges over the Thames.

d Most of the mountains are in the south of Europe. There aren't many mountains in the north.

e The Volga passes through one country. The Danube passes through 10 countries.

2 **Read the blog post about a trip on a river cruise and answer the questions.**

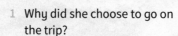

Dream holiday

I just got back from a five-day cruise on the Danube. It's a trip I've dreamt of taking since I can remember. I did my research, read some books and even asked a few friends who had done it before for advice. When I saw the boat, I was a bit disappointed. It's not that it looked unsafe; it just looked normal. Luckily, once I stepped on board and saw the inside, it was just like I had dreamt it. We ate half our meals in the boat's restaurant and the rest in the cities we stopped at. All the food was so delicious, I can't even choose a favourite. The views from the top deck were amazing and the whole day was planned out. There was no stress thinking about what to do next. The trip was fantastic; it's impossible to say what was best!

1 Why did she choose to go on the trip?
  a A friend recommended it.
  b It's something she has always wanted to do.
  c She read about it in a book.

2 What was her first impression of the boat?
  a It looked unsafe.
  b It didn't seem very special.
  c It was just as she imagined.

3 How did she feel about the food on board?
  a It was better than the food in the cities.
  b It was just as good as the food in the cities.
  c It was worse than the food in the cities.

4 What was her favourite part about the cruise?
  a The stress-free travel.
  b The views from the boat.
  c She can't choose just one.

26

> Encourage pupils to revise the unit content using the techniques from page 81.

Content Review

1 Draw the outline of Europe. Add five dots for capital cities and five physical features, but no labels. Ask and answer with a partner.

> What's the name of this capital city?

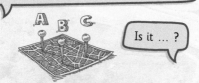

> Is it ... ?

> What are these mountains called?

> They're the ...

Assessment link

For more Unit 2 activities go to page 80.

2 Copy and complete the table.

	Land boundaries	Water boundaries	Five mountain ranges	Five rivers
Europe				
Spain				

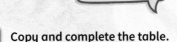 **FINALE**

- In groups, combine your information and ideas to create the perfect class trip.
- The trip will be a week long. You must visit at least three capital cities, travel once on a river and visit a mountain range.
- Create a slide presentation to propose the trip to the class. Show where the trip will go, what you will see and why it is the perfect trip. The class will vote for the best trip.

27

> Put pupils in small groups of three or four. Give them time in class to share their ideas and plan a trip using the criteria in the book. They can prepare the presentation at home, but remind them to assign work to everyone in the group.

Content Review answers

1 Pupils' own answers

2 Europe

Land boundaries: Ural Mountains; Caucasus Mountains

Water boundaries: Arctic Ocean; Atlantic Ocean; Mediterranean Sea; Black Sea; Caspian Sea

Five mountain ranges: (five of the following) Ural Mountains; Caucasus Mountains; The Alps; Pyrenees; Carpathian Mountains; Scandanavian Mountains, Balkan Mountains, Apennine Mountains

Five rivers: (five of the following) Volga; Thames; Seine; Rhine; Danube Pechora, Northern Dvina, Western Dvina, Ural, Don, Dnieper, Oder, Elbe, Rhône, Po, Tiber, Loire, Thames

Spain

Land boundaries: Pyrenees; Portugal; Andorra; Morocco; the UK (Gibraltar)

Water boundaries: Mar Cantábrico; Atlantic Ocean; Mediterranean Sea

Five mountain ranges: Sistema Ibérico; Sistema Central; Cordillera Cantábrico; Sistemas Béticos; Sierra Morena

Five rivers: Duero; Tajo; Ebro; Guadiana; Guadalquivir

Think about it answers

1 The Ural and Caucasus Mountains.

2 There are around 50.

3 Arctic Ocean, Atlantic Ocean, Mediterranean Sea, Black Sea, Caspian Sea

4 All the countries and capitals covered on page 20–21.

5 It is 3,530 km long.

6 Paris and the Seine; London and the Thames; Lisbon and the Tajo; Rome and the Tiber; Budapest, Vienna or Bratislava and the Danube.

7 It passes through Germany, Austria, Slovakia, Hungary, Croatia, Serbia, Bulgaria, Romania, Moldova, Ukraine.

8 They are the Alps, Caucasus, Carpathian, Pyrenees and Ural Mountains.

9 They pass through France, Italy, Switzerland, Liechtenstein, Austria, Germany and Slovenia.

10 It is Mount Elbrus in the Caucasus Mountains.

Think harder answers

1 The continent forms an enormous peninsula, but it is covered with a number of smaller peninsulas too.

2 There isn't a large body of water separating Europe and Asia.

3 Many countries that are near each other have very similar flags.

4 Most countries have access to the sea. It was vital for transport of people and goods in the past and still is important for trade and commerce.

5 Moscow, London, Berlin, Madrid, Rome, Paris. Example answers: climate, employment, quality of life.

6 Example answers: Rivers and mountains made excellent defense positions so many armies couldn't cross them. They created easily markable areas.

7 It provides transport, defence and resources, but makes construction of roads and travel within the city more difficult and has the possibility of flooding.

8 Most of the rivers in Europe are navigable by boat while Spain has very few that can be used for transport due to its climate and geography.

9 Pupils' own answers

10 Example answers. *Tour de France* in the Alps and Pyrenees; *Giro de Italia* bike race; *Vuelta de España* through the mountains of Spain; The *Boat Race* on the River Thames

UNIT 2 TRACKLIST

3

SPAIN IN THE 19TH CENTURY

Learning objectives

By the end of this unit, pupils will have achieved a greater understanding of the following concepts:

- The French Revolution as the beginning of the Modern Age
- The uprising of 2 May, 1808 as the beginning of the War of Independence
- Important events and people of the War of Independence
- The creation of the first liberal constitution in Cádiz in 1812
- The resistance to liberalism and the Carlist wars
- The independence of Spain's American territories in the early 19th century
- The works of Francisco de Goya

Competences

This unit covers the following competences:

- Linguistic competence
- Mathematical and basic competences in science and technology
- Digital competence
- Learning to learn
- Cultural awareness and expression

Key vocabulary

War of Independence: alliance, ally, army, battle, Carlos IV, French Revolution, *guerrillas*, Joseph Bonaparte, Modern Age, Napoleon Bonaparte, peasant, power, revolt, rise up, siege, traditionalism, treaty, uprising, *valido*

Constitution of 1812: constitutional monarch, delegate, democracy, election, equality, freedom, freedom of expression, freedom of press

Reign of Fernando VII: absolute monarch, absolutists, Carlist war, Carlists, crisis, instability, Isabel II, Liberal Triennium, Liberalism, Liberals, Maria Cristina, regent

Goya: bright, court painter, dark, horror, Impressionist, merry, wealth

Internet: advertisements, Information Age, keyword, trustworthy

Cambridge English Qualifications practice

You will find *B1 Preliminary for Schools* activity types in the following exercises:
Pupil's Book, Page 40, Activity 2 – Listening Part 4
Pupil's Book, Page 40, Activity 3 –Writing Part 2
Activity Book, Page 15, Activity 5 – Writing Part 1
Activity Book, Page 18, Activity 11 – Reading Part 5

Throughout this unit, you will find the following *B1 Preliminary for Schools* vocabulary:
advertisement, against, army, battle, bright, century, dark, declare, election, fair, find out, give up, horror, modern, nearby, occupation, popular, power, progress, society, success, suffer, talent, technique, terrible, think about, traditional, trust

Materials needed for *Find out more*

- access to the internet

Materials needed for other activities

- blank paper or card   • poster making supplies   • access to the internet

Explore

The *Explore* project encourages pupils to create a super-sized timeline by interpreting past events in modern ways as if they were social media events. Pupils draw what they think events would have looked liked, write responses to events as if they were living then, create posts commemorating important days and think about how to arrange all the events on a timeline.

The different *Explore* stages focus on the following skills:

- autonomous research
- creative expression
- drawing historical events
- organising events in history
- writing informal comments

Digital Lab 6 Social Science

Interactive activities

Flashcards

Song: *Dos de Mayo*

Video documentary: Built in the 19th century

Objective

Pupils will take an overall look at the first half of the Modern Age and define some important terminology of the era.

Key vocabulary

absolute monarch, constitutional monarch, crisis, instability, Liberalism, Traditionalism

Warm up

- Tell pupils that we have arrived at the last era of human history to study: *The Modern Age*. Draw a long timeline on the board with five divisions. Have pupils brainstorm in groups to see how many time periods can be correctly labelled: *Pre-History, Ancient History, The Middle Ages, The Early Modern Age, The Modern Age*. Pupils copy the timeline into their notebooks.

Main concepts

- Using the images on the page, have pupils brainstorm what events they think will be covered in the unit. Pupils share ideas with the class.

- Play *Truth or lie*. In groups, pupils have one minute to study the illustration before closing their books. Next, one pupil opens the book and describes something: *There is a man with a French flag* or *The word liberal is written on a paper*. The group must decide if it is a true description or if the pupil has made it up.

Liberalism: Political ideas that focus on individual freedoms and rights and social progress. It supports constitutions and limited governments.

Traditionalism: Political ideas that support the old ways such as absolute monarchy and limited freedoms.

Absolute monarch: A ruler from a royal family that has complete power and control over their country.

Constitutional monarch: A ruler from a royal family that has limited powers set by a constitution.

Can you define the words written on the sticky notes?

S ng
Dos de Mayo

TRADITIONALISM

CARLISTS

ABSOLUTE MONARCH

3

4

5

6

CONSTITUTIONAL MONARCH

D CUMENTARY
Built in the 19th century

Explore

Interpret the events of the 19th century in a modern way by creating social media posts and comments. You will:

- investigate important events and people.
- identify new revolutionary ideas and their effects.
- study the work of Francisco de Goya.
- create a super-sized timeline summarising the era.

29

Remind pupils that on the last stage they will combine all their work with the rest of the class, so they must keep everything organised and neat. Discuss how social media affects us positively and negatively regarding the spread of information, rumours and news coverage.

Learn more

- On the board write the dates: *1788–1808, 1808–1833, 1833–1868, 1870–1873*. Have pupils guess which leaders shown on the page ruled during those timespans.

Song
This song focuses on the events of *Dos de Mayo*. It can be used on pages 32–33.

Documentary
The documentary takes pupils on a tour of Spanish cities, focusing in particular on Madrid and its architecture from the 19th century. It can be used on pages 40–41 to review the time period as a whole.

Tip

Look at the desk in the picture. Ask for adjectives to describe the desk. Elicit words like *unorganised*, *chaotic*, *messy*. Ask if the desk is a workspace where a lot of work can get done. Explain to pupils that the desk represents the era, it was unstable and little progress was made.

Objective

Pupils will learn about the events and effect of the French Revolution and identify it as the beginning of the Modern Era.

Key vocabulary

battle, democracy, equality, freedom, French Revolution, liberty, Modern Age, Napoleon Bonaparte, peasant, rise up

Warm up

- Ask pupils what they remember about feudalism: *Nobles owned all the land. Peasants lived on the land and had to pay the nobles with work and a share of the produce.* Explain that the inequalities of the system were the basis of the French Revolution.

Main concepts

- Have pupils look at the illustration and discuss what is happening and what they recognise. Why is there a crown flying though the air? Who are the peasants fighting? Why are there armies surrounding France?

Learn more

- Ask pupils: *What would you do if you were ruler of Spain? Fight against a very powerful French army, ally with France or ally with England, your long-time rival?* Have pupils prepare a minute-long explanation about their decision.

They were imprisoned and then executed by guillotine.

A revolution in France and the beginning of Carlos IV's reign.

WHAT WAS HAPPENING IN 1789?

Discover...
how the French Revolution affected all of Europe.

The **French Revolution** began in 1789 when the peasant class rose up against the old feudalist system.

The uprising in France succeeded, absolute monarchy ended and a government based on equality and freedom was established.

Kings from nearby countries declared war on France to stop the new government and its ideas.

What happened to the King and Queen of France?

The new French government experienced many problems, but the French Army, under General **Napoleon Bonaparte**, won battle after battle all over Europe.

When Napoleon returned from war in 1799, he declared the revolution over and made himself Emperor of France and absolute ruler.

This period was chaotic and violent, and it didn't provide France with democracy, but its actions and ideas changed the course of history and marked the beginning of the **Modern Age** in Western Europe.

Find out what the Modern Age is called in your language.

Same time, different place:
As the revolution was taking place in France, Carlos IV was in his first year as king after the death of his father, Carlos III. The French Revolution caused difficulties for all the royal families in Europe.

30

Edad Contemporánea

For next lesson ... access to the internet

> Here's the hidden object!

HOW DO YOU DO RESEARCH ONLINE?

Find out more...

Discover... how to find and evaluate online information.

Background: We live in the Information Age where we can find out almost anything we want, but how do we know if this information can be trusted or is fair? We need to think about where the information comes from and why it is there.

Materials: access to the internet

Part 1: **Keys to a good internet search**
Make your search more effective by choosing your words carefully. These words are called **keywords**. Search for answers to the questions using one keyword, then try with more. Can you find the answers? What words gave the best results?

- Were Carlos IV and Louis XVI related?
- Which French revolutionary was killed in the bath?
- Was Napoleon Bonaparte short?

Part 2: **Evaluating websites**
What makes a website trustworthy? Look at the checklist and brainstorm two more questions that you can ask yourself when evaluating a website.

- Is the website full of advertisements?
- Can you find the author or organisation that made the site?
- Does the site only tell one side of the story?

Task: Imagine your school wants to eliminate breaktime. You will need facts and information from trusted sources to make a good argument that it should stay.

Using the techniques from Parts 1 and 2, find three websites to send to your teacher on the importance of breaktime and why it is necessary.

31

Objective

Pupils will learn how to search the internet and evaluate the information they find.

Key vocabulary

advertisements, Information Age, keyword, trustworthy

Warm up

- Write the following on the board: *.com/.es; .edu; .gov/.gob; .org* and *.blogspot* and ask pupils how they are different. Explain that *.edu* is for universities, *.gov/.gob* are official government websites and *.org* belongs to organisations. Then, ask pupils to think about what that tells us about a website.

Main concepts

- Have pupils create a list titled *Tips for finding good information* to share with other pupils and another list titled *Trustworthy websites* to fill out whenever they find a good website. They can post them in the computer lab or around the school.

Learn more

- There are great websites and videos with tips and tricks for using search engines. Have pupils search online and present to the class two or three tips they discovered.

Objective

Pupils will identify the beginning of the War of Independence as the event of *Dos de Mayo* and study the events leading up to it.

Key vocabulary

alliance, ally with, Carlos IV, Joseph Bonaparte, revolt, rise up, 2 May 1808, treaty, uprising, *valido*, War of Independence

Warm up

- Play *Broken telephone* using sentences from the page. Write the reported sentence from the last pupils on the board and have pupils search the page to find any mistakes.

- Explain that most information was spread by word of mouth in the past and ask how it could lead to panic, misinformation, rumours, anger, etc. Ask: *How could this have affected Dos de Mayo and the War of Independence?*

Main concepts

- Draw a square on the board and inside write: *Godoy signing the Treaty of Fontainebleau*. Then, draw an arrow leading to an empty box. Tell pupils to create a flowchart leading up to the War of Independence. When they finish, have pupils say an event to a classmate while the other pupil responds with what happened next.

The uprising of the 2 May, 1808

Treaty of Fontainebleau

WHAT STARTED THE WAR OF INDEPENDENCE?

With Napoleon dominating Europe in battle, **Carlos IV** and his *valido* decided that they should ally with France and Napoleon rather than fight against them. The alliance failed and a war against France followed.

Discover...
the events that led to war.

M_Godoy Making big plans! 1807

Manuel Godoy was a young general who became a favourite of Carlos IV. As Prime Minister, he signed a secret treaty with France to conquer and divide up Portugal together.

What was the treaty called?

Instead of just passing through Spain, the French forces started to occupy fortresses in the north and centre of the country. The people were angry about the French occupation and grew tired of Godoy's policies and revolted. They captured Godoy and forced Carlos IV to pass the crown to his son, **Fernando VII**.

Where did the uprising take place?

Anonymous We want Fernando VII!
19 March 1808. Aranjuez

Napoleon invited Carlos IV and Fernando VII to France for a conference, but when they got there, he forced them to give up the throne and imprisoned them. He made his brother, **Joseph Bonaparte**, King of Spain.

N_Bonaparte My brother is king, nothing can stop me!
August 1808

32

In Aranjuez.

The French soldiers executed the people of Madrid who had fought against them.

With the king in France and French soldiers in Madrid, the people of Madrid decided to take action. They rose up against the soldiers on the **2 May 1808**, setting off a day of terrible fighting in the streets.

The uprising was stopped, but the stories of the heroism of the people of Madrid and the cruelty of the French soldiers inspired others to join the fight against Napoleon. This began **The War of Independence**.

What happened on 3 May 1808?

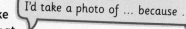

What difficulties does the land create for anyone trying to conquer Spain?

Explore — STAGE 1

- Nowadays, all major events are recorded on social media with photos or videos. Imagine you were at one of the historical events above and had a mobile phone to record it.

I'd take a photo of ... because ...

- In your notebook, write what photo you would take to post online and why you chose it. Then draw what you think it would look like. Use the paintings above for help.

Give pupils time in class to share ideas. Encourage them to draw different events to their classmates and to add social media images like time stamps, hashtags and emojis. The drawing can be done either at home or in class. Pupils should use the paintings on the page to help with ideas about what people wore and what they looked like.

33

For next lesson ...
access to the internet

Learn more

- Quiz pupils by describing an action and having pupils name who did it. For example; *Rose up against French forces.* (People of Madrid); *Named his brother king of Spain* (Napoleon). Have pupils create questions to ask each other.

Tip

Try an experiment on how information spreads by telling pupils an interesting fact about yourself and instructing them to inform only one person from another class. Have the pupils conduct a survey the next day to see how many pupils know the piece of information and if it changed at all.

Spain is a very mountainous country with mountain ranges running north to south and east to west. This makes it difficult for foreign armies to travel and provides excellent areas to build defence points such as forts and castles.

Objective

Pupils will discover the important events and people of the War of Independence. They will study the Constitution of 1812 and its creation. They will associate the first quarter of the 19th century with the loss of most of Spain's overseas territories.

Key vocabulary

army, Constitution of 1812, delegate, election, freedom of expression, freedom of press, *guerrillas*, power, siege

Warm up

- Draw a table on the board with two columns: *Before* and *During*. Have pupils try to remember the actions leading up to the war with a partner and add them to the board. Ask them if they know anything that happened during the war and add it to the board.

Main concepts

- Using their new search abilities, give pupils ten minutes to research one person and one event online. They need to write a brief description to present to the class.

> The Constitution of 1812 was written. Most of Spain's overseas territories gained their independence. Napoleon was defeated.

> Pupils' own answers

WHAT HAPPENED DURING THE WAR?

Discover...
the major events and key figures of the war.

During the war, the regular Spanish Army had little success, but small groups of fighters called *guerrillas* caused problems for the French Army with their unique fighting style. With the help of the British and Portuguese Armies, Napoleon was defeated in 1814 and Fernando VII returned to the Spanish throne.

The Siege of Zaragoza

Augustina de Aragón

Men and women all over the country fought during the War of Independence. What do you know about these battles and people?

> Find out more about them and other events during the war.

Pedro Velarde y Santillán

The Battle of Bailén

The Siege of Zaragoza (1808 and 1809): a two-month long defence of the city.

Augustina de Aragón: A women delivering food to soldiers saw they were defeated and retreating, so she fired the cannons herself.

Siege of Gerona (1809): The army and people fought for seven months to defend the city.

Pedro Velarde y Santillán: A captain who fought with the people against the French on 2 May. He died fighting that day.

Arthur Wellesley (*Duke of Wellington*): He led the British troops in the victory over France.

The Battle of Bailén (1808): One of the first victories against a Napoleonic army.

Because it was signed on 19 March, the day of *San José*.

While most of the country was under French occupation, Cádiz was still under Spanish control. Using new liberal ideas spread by the French Revolution, delegates wrote **The Constitution of 1812**. It was approved on 19 March 1812.

It created a **constitutional monarchy** with Fernando VII as king but limited the king's power. It was the first constitution in Spanish history. It granted all Spanish people equality under the law, freedom of press, freedom of expression and the right to choose their representatives through elections.

Why is the Constitution sometimes called *La Pepa*?

The independence of Spain's American territories

Same time, different place:

During the War of Independence and the reign of Fernando VII, the inhabitants of Spain's **American territories** demanded independence. All the political battles, wars and instability left Spain unable to defend its territories. By the end of Fernando's reign in 1833, only Cuba, Puerto Rico and the Philippines were under Spanish control.

 **STAGE 2**

• Paintings and monuments were created to honour and commemorate people and events. Today, most news websites have a *Today in history* section to remind us of these events. Research information on a battle and a key figure from the War of Independence.

• Create two short *Today in history* posts with text and images to commemorate them.

35

Objective

Pupils will analyse how the resistance to liberalism brought instability, fighting and little progress.

Key vocabulary

absolutists, Carlist war, Carlists, Isabel II, Liberal Triennium, liberals, María Cristina, regent, republic

Warm up

- Draw two stick figures having a tug of war on the board. Write *liberal* on one and *absolutist* on the other. Explain that they represent the political battle that faced Spain for the next 40 years. Power moved from one side to another, but just like tug of war, there was little progress.

Main concepts

- Write the word *El Deseado* on the board and tell pupils it was a nickname for Fernando VII, although it didn't last long. Elicit what it means in English and ask why he was called that and why people stopped calling him that so quickly. *(He declared the Constitution illegal and imprisoned many who had fought for his return.)*

- Play *Liberal or Absolutist?* Pupils say sentences such as: *I believe the power of a king should be limited; Women shouldn't rule a country;* and the rest of the class decides if they are a *liberal* or an *absolutist*.

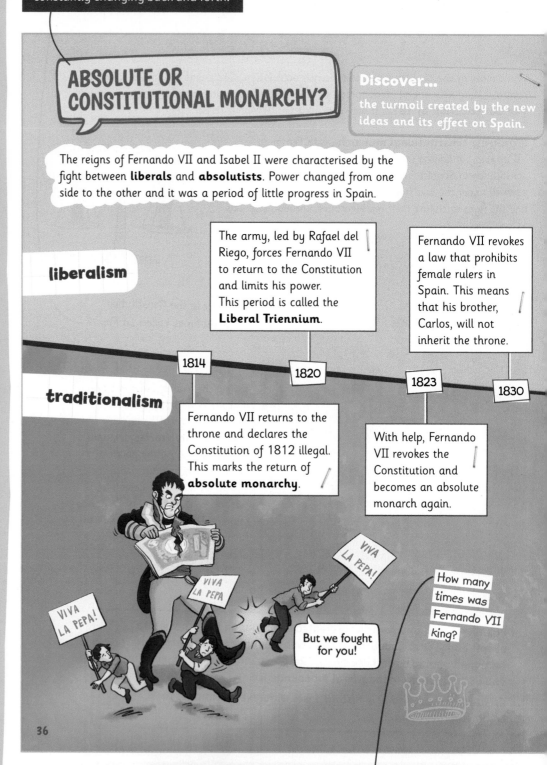

A country without a king or queen, usually governed by elected representatives of the people and a president.

As a true republic it lasted 11 months and had four presidents. It was followed by a year when the government wasn't ruled by a monarch but had supreme power. The monarchy was restored almost two years after the Republic was declared.

Learn more

- Play *Who am I?* to review the unit. Pupils take a piece of paper and cut it into four squares. They write an important person, event or thing from any page in the unit on each square. Now, in groups of four, pupils exchange cards without looking at them. A pupil then places the card on their forehead while the other pupils describe it until it can be guessed.

Tip

To help pupils organise all the information encourage them to create a simplified timeline with their own summaries of the events covered on pages 30–37. Encourage them to use different colours and symbols to keep it organised and easy to study.

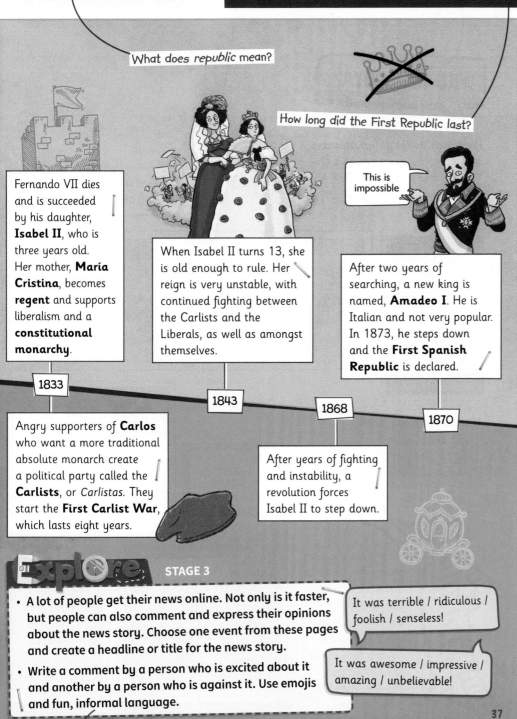

What does *republic* mean?

How long did the First Republic last?

This is impossible

Fernando VII dies and is succeeded by his daughter, **Isabel II**, who is three years old. Her mother, **María Cristina**, becomes **regent** and supports liberalism and a **constitutional monarchy**.

When Isabel II turns 13, she is old enough to rule. Her reign is very unstable, with continued fighting between the Carlists and the Liberals, as well as amongst themselves.

After two years of searching, a new king is named, **Amadeo I**. He is Italian and not very popular. In 1873, he steps down and the **First Spanish Republic** is declared.

1833

1843

1868

1870

Angry supporters of **Carlos** who want a more traditional absolute monarch create a political party called the **Carlists**, or *Carlistas*. They start the **First Carlist War**, which lasts eight years.

After years of fighting and instability, a revolution forces Isabel II to step down.

Explore
STAGE 3

- A lot of people get their news online. Not only is it faster, but people can also comment and express their opinions about the news story. Choose one event from these pages and create a headline or title for the news story.
- Write a comment by a person who is excited about it and another by a person who is against it. Use emojis and fun, informal language.

It was terrible / ridiculous / foolish / senseless!

It was awesome / impressive / amazing / unbelievable!

37

Pupils may need help with writing a headline. Show them examples online and explain they are meant to grab attention. Pupils may respond better if you describe it as *click bait* or *the interesting titles of links or videos online to get you to click on them*. Discuss online comments, how they are used and their vocabulary and writing style. Point out that it is informal and often very excited or angry.

Objective

Pupils will learn about the life and works of Francisco de Goya and analyse the changes in his work.

Key vocabulary

bright, court painter, dark, horror, Impressionists, merry, power, wealth

Warm up

- Before opening the books, show pupils a picture of Goya and ask if anyone knows who it is. Tell them it is Francisco de Goya and ask if anyone can name one of his paintings. Elicit answers by giving clues.

Main concepts

- Explain to pupils that some of the paintings seen throughout the unit were painted by Goya. Using what they've learned about Goya and the paintings on these pages as a guide, have pupils hunt through the unit to find the other Goya paintings and decide in which frame they belong. Pupils share their answers with a partner and explain their reasons.

One of the greatest painters of his time who worked with royalty, painted historic scenes and daily life in Spain and influenced many artists after him.

Francisco Goya y Lucientes (Self-Portrait), Plate 1 of *Los Caprichos* is on page 31. The Caprichos are a group of 80 works produced by Goya during this time period. This work is in the National Galleries of Scotland.

WHO WAS GOYA?

Discover...

the great talent and techniques of Francisco de Goya.

Francisco de Goya y Lucientes is considered one of the greatest painters of his time. He lived from 1746 to 1828. During his life, his style changed to reflect the events that were occurring at the time.

Find a self-portrait of Goya hidden in the unit.

Painting on loan

His early paintings show bright and merry scenes of daily life. They influenced the Impressionist movement.

Painting on loan

He became the court painter for Carlos III and Carlos IV. He was excellent at showing the wealth and power of the royalty, but did not alter his subjects to make them more beautiful.

38

Learn more

• Have pupils write a review as if they were an art critic. Pupils should choose a painting and say what they think of it, what they think Goya wanted to express and how much they think it would cost to buy it today.

Painting on loan

Painting on loan

The suffering and violence during the War of Independence greatly affected Goya's work. His paintings show the real horror and brutality of war and are pessimistic and critical of society.

Affected by illness, loss of hearing and upset about the political situation, Goya's work became dark. These painting are called his *Black Paintings* and were painted on the walls of his house. He didn't title them or show them to the public.

Find the missing Goya paintings in the unit and decide where they belong.

What is your favourite piece of Goya's work? Why? Discuss with a partner.

Tip

Art can be difficult for some pupils to engage with so have pupils think of it as if they were posts on social media: showing their feelings, recording events and drawing their friends, just like people do now with smartphones.

 **STAGE 4**

• Goya changed the colour palette to give his paintings different moods and feelings. What other techniques did he use?

• Look through the unit and group the events that are related into different time periods. What would you name the time periods? What colours or symbols would you use to represent each one?

I'd call this time period …

To represent this time period, I'd use …

• Write your ideas in your notebook to use later.

39

Have pupils work in small groups to elicit better and more creative ideas. Every few minutes stop the class and ask for their best ideas and write them on the board and then have the groups continue working. Remind them to record their ideas to use later.

Pupils' own answers

Language Review answers

1 b The Constitution of 1812 limited the king's powers.

c The Constitution was made illegal in 1814 by Fernando VII.

d A treaty with Napoleon was signed by Godoy to conquer Portugal.

e The Carlists fought many battles against Isabel II.

f Etchings as well as paintings were done by Goya.

2 1 b

2 c

3 a

4 c

5 b

> This activity gives pupils practice of *B1 Preliminary for Schools* Listening Part 4.

3 Pupils' own answers

> This activity gives pupils practice of *B1 Preliminary for Schools* Writing Part 2.

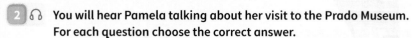

Language Review

1 In your notebook, change the sentences from active to passive or passive to active.

a Goya painted many beautiful works of art.
   Many beautiful works of art were painted by Goya.
b The king's powers were limited by the Constitution of 1812.
c Fernando VII made the Constitution illegal in 1814.
d Godoy signed a treaty with Napoleon to conquer Portugal.
e Many battles were fought by the Carlists against Isabel II.
f Goya did etchings as well as paintings.

2 🎧 You will hear Pamela talking about her visit to the Prado Museum. For each question choose the correct answer.

1 She finally visited the Prado because …
   a her grandmother took her.
   b she went with a class trip.
   c she went for her birthday.
2 How did she first feel when she entered?
   a Excited to see it all.
   b Nervous about breaking something.
   c Impressed by its size.

3 Which painting was her favourite?
   a *El Parasol.*
   b *Dos de Mayo.*
   c She couldn't choose just one.
4 How did she feel about Goya's Black Paintings?
   a Sad for him.
   b Interested in the theme.
   c Scared.
5 What does she plan to do next?
   a Return to the Prado.
   b Visit the Reina Sofía.
   c Take art classes.

3 Your English teacher has asked you to write a story. Your story must begin with this sentence: *It was 1808 and I was 12 years old.* Write 100 words or more.

40

Content Review

Content Review answers

Content Review

✓ **Assessment link**
For more Unit 3 activities go to page 82.

1 Choose the correct answer.

a Who fought two wars against the reign of Isabel II?

Carlists   Guerrillas   Liberals

b Where was the Constitution of 1812 written?

Madrid   Cádiz   Paris

c What started the War of Independence?

The treaty of Fontainebleau   The uprising on 2 May 1808   The Battle of Victoria

d Which countries helped Spain in the War of Independence?

The United States and Portugal   Britain and Italy   Portugal and Britain

e What wasn't established by the Constitution of 1812?

Freedom of expression and press   A republic   A constitutional monarchy

2 Match the leaders to the events.

Joseph I   Carlos IV   Isabel II   Fernando VII

a The Constitution of 1812 was written.

b The French Revolution began and marked the beginning of the Modern Age in the West.

c The Constitution of 1812 was declared illegal.

d The Revolution of 1868 happened.

e Most of the territories in America gained independence from Spain.

f Manuel Godoy signed a treaty with Napoleon.

Explore — FINALE

- Time for a timeline! As a class, choose the best place for a super-sized timeline to go. Decide how to divide up the timeline so it uses all the space.

- Make the timeline more interesting by using your ideas from Stage 4 to create time periods with different colours and symbols.

- When the timeline is made, you can place your work from Stages 1, 2, and 3 on it. How does it look? Are any major events missing? Add more posts.

Let's divide the timeline into …

This event needs to be placed in …

41

Content Review answers

1 a Carlists

  b Cádiz

  c The uprising of 2 May 1808

  d Portugal and Britain

  e A republic

2 a Joseph I

  b Carlos IV

  c Fernando VII

  d Isabel II

  e Fernando VII

  f Carlos IV

Think about it answers

1 The French Revolution began in 1789 and Carlos IV was King of Spain.

2 Manuel Godoy signed the Treaty of Fontainebleau with France.

3 The War of Independence started with the uprising of 2 May, 1808 in Madrid.

4 Possible answers: The Siege of Zaragoza, The Siege of Gerona, The Battle of Bailén, Augustina de Arágon, Pedro Velarde y Santillán.

5 It was written in Cádiz. It created a constitutional monarchy, gave equality under the law and freedom of speech.

6 He declared it illegal and imprisoned its supporters.

7 Most gained their independence because Spain couldn't defend them due to the instability and fighting in Spain.

8 They were upset that Isabel II was made the monarch and not Carlos. They fought civil wars against her government.

9 Carlos IV, Fernando VII, Joseph I, Fernando VII, Maria Cristina (regent), Isabel II, Amadeo I

10 Possible answers: *El Columpio, El Quitasol, La Pradera de San Isidro, La familia de Carlos IV, El Dos de Mayo en Madrid, El Tres de Mayo en Madrid, Aquelarre*

Think harder answers

1 It spread enlightenment ideas throughout the world, inspired revolutions in South America, began wars between monarchies and Napoleon.

2 Napoleon's government was anti-monarchy but to go against him meant Spain had to ally with England.

3 They used new fighting techniques that the French had never seen before.

4 Pupils' own answers

5 Pupils' own answers

6 Pupils' own answers

7 Pupils' own answers

8 Fernando VII had an absolute monarchy and Isabel II had a constitutional monarchy. Both of their reigns were marked by instability and fighting.

9 Instability and constant change don't allow a government or society to progress.

10 Possible answers: The Prado in Madrid; Meadows Museum in Texas; The M.E.T. in New York; National Gallery, UK; Zaragoza Museum, Spain

UNIT 3 TRACKLIST

4 THE PATH TO MODERN SPAIN

Learning objectives

By the end of this unit, pupils will have achieved a greater understanding of the following concepts:

- The modernisation of Spain during the Restoration
- Important cultural and political figures of the Restoration
- The loss of the last overseas territories
- The beginning and end of the Second Republic, the Civil War and life in Spain post war
- Important dates and events of the current democracy

Competences

This unit covers the following competences:

- Linguistic competence
- Mathematical competence and basic competences in science and technology
- Digital competence
- Learning to learn
- Social and civic competences
- Cultural awareness and expression

Key vocabulary

The Restoration: agriculture, bourgeoisie, capitalist, classes, dynasty, economic growth, industrial, middle class, modernisation, nobility, rural, stability, *turno pacifico*, upper class, unions, urban, working class

The Second Republic: education reforms, labour movement, land reforms, mandatory, social reform

The Civil War: aid, generals, military coup, military, militia, nationalist, republican

Dictatorship: absolute power, autarky, censor, civil liberties, economic crisis, emigrate, illegal, rationing, repress, restricted

Democracy: appoint, constitution, democratic elections, Prime Minister, referendum, strike, transition, vote

Other: adverts, convince, influence, propaganda

Cambridge English Qualifications practice

You will find **B1 Preliminary for Schools** activity types in the following exercises:
Pupil's Book, Page 54, Activity 3 – Speaking Part 3
Activity Book, Page 24, Activity 12 – Reading Part 6

Throughout this unit, you will find the following **B1 Preliminary for Schools** vocabulary: advance, advert, agree, aid, business, convince, cost, decision, economic, education, improve, lack, own, owner, power, religion, replace, result, return, strike, union, vote

Materials needed for *Find out more*

- poster
- paper
- paints
- pens
- scissors
- glue
- craft materials

Materials needed for other activities

- index cards
- image of the *Guernica* by Picasso

Explore

The *Explore* project has pupils create their own digital history museum. They profile important figures, find artefacts and photos online, interview people who lived through the transition into democracy and take the class on a tour. The different *Explore* stages practise the following skills:

- researching online
- describing past events
- profiling historic figures
- autonomous research
- using photographs to show life in the past
- conducting an interview
- creating a digital exhibition
- public speaking

Digital Lab 6 Social Science

Interactive activities

Flashcards

Song: *All these new things*

Video documentary: *The Madrid Metro*

UNIT 4
PAGES 42–43

Objective

Pupils will be introduced to the different eras of the 20th century in Spain and their characteristics.

Key vocabulary

Democratic Spain, Franco's Dictatorship, repression, The Civil War, The Restoration, The Second Republic

Warm up

- Ask pupils what the word *modern* means. Write *modern Spain* on the board and ask pupils what they think makes a modern country and make a mind map with their ideas. You can add subcategories such as *technology*, *society*, *government*.

Main concepts

- After the puzzle pieces have been identified, pupils write the name of each in their notebook and list as many things as they can from each piece. They then share their answers with their classmates.

- Play *I spy*. In small groups, one pupil describes something on the page by saying, '*I spy with my little eye …*' while the rest of the group searches for it. The first to find it gets to describe in the next round.

1: The Restoration: Lower-class workers are working in the factory. There is a steam train representing modernisation. The capitalist class system is shown with the upper classes standing in a separate area. Some men are waiting to vote and are being told what to do. Alfonso XII is king.

2: The Second Republic: Some men and women are queuing to vote. Boys and girls are going to school together.

4 THE PATH TO MODERN SPAIN

Look and discuss…

Do you recognise the time periods represented by the puzzle pieces?

VOTE HERE

VOTE HERE

Another period of fighting, repression and instability finally ended in a modern Spain for all its citizens.

1 The Restoration; 2 The Second Republic; 3 The Civil War; 4 Franco's dictatorship; 5 Democratic Spain

42

3: The Civil War: There are destroyed buildings and infrastructure. A warplane is flying overhead. There are uniformed soldiers and militia fighting each other.

4: Franco's dictatorship: Some rebuilding is being done. There are people queueing for food with ration books. Police officers have stopped people who were protesting.

5: Democratic Spain. There is a peaceful demonstration and children playing in a square. There is a modern factory. Felipe VI is King. He and the Prime Minister are holding the Constitution.

Inform pupils they will be creating a digital presentation and discuss different computer programs they can use. Give some examples and instructions for making slides, making them easy to read and not distracting. Ask if anyone is familiar with a program and have them explain how and what to use. If pupils don't have access to a computer at home, create time at school.

Learn more

- To review new vocabulary and practise speaking skills, instruct pupils to imagine they are in one of the pieces. In groups, pupils then create a script talking about what they can see or what they are doing. Have them perform it and ask the class to decide what era they are in.

Song

This song focuses on all the new ideas and technology that appeared during this era. It can be used on pages 42–43.

Documentary

The documentary focuses on the Madrid Metro, which was inaugurated by Alfonso XIII in 1919. It can be used on page 46.

Tip

Return to this page before or after each lesson to review. Focus on the puzzle piece that represents the lesson and ask the pupils if they notice any more details now that they have studied the era.

Objective

Pupils will learn about the Restoration and important political and cultural figures at the time.

Key vocabulary

economic growth, stability, *turno pacífico*, military coup, dictatorship, dynasty

Warm up

- Tell pupils that the Restoration restored the Bourbon dynasty. Have pupils begin with the *Look back* feature and review the Bourbon rulers from Unit 3. As a class, create a large family tree on the board adding *Alfonso XII, María Cristina* and *Alfonso XIII*. Ask pupils if anyone can add any more names from what they studied last year: *Felipe V, Louis I, Fernando VI, Carlos III.*

Main concepts

- Have pupils look over the lesson and find three events and their effects. In pairs, one pupil says one of the events to see if their partner can say the effect or vice-versa. For example: **Pupil A**: *Alfonso XII died before his son was born.* **Pupil B**: *His wife, María Cristina ruled as regent.* **Pupil B**: *Alfonso XII was named king.* **Pupil A**: *The Bourbon dynasty was restored to power.*

The reign of the Bourbon Dynasty.

Alfonso XII died while María Cristina was pregnant with Alfonso XIII.

WHAT WAS RESTORED DURING THE RESTORATION?

Discover... what led to the most stable period in Spain in one hundred years.

The **Restoration** was the return of the Bourbon dynasty to power. It was a time of economic growth and stability, but it came at the cost of democracy and freedom.

Alfonso XII's reign followed the First Republic. He was a popular constitutional ruler for ten years, but he died at the age of 27.

His son, **Alfonso XIII**, became king the day he was born, but his mother, **María Cristina**, ruled as regent until 1902 when he turned 16.

Why aren't there any photos of the family together?

| 1875–1885 | 1885–1902 |

ALFON SO XII MARÍA CRIS TINA AL

Political stability was achieved by the **turno pacífico**, a system created by **Antonio Cánovas del Castillo** that decided the result of elections in advance.

How did the *turno pacífico* work?

Look back

Who were the Bourbon rulers before the Restoration?

Felipe V, Fernando VI, Carlos III, Carlos IV, Fernando VII, Isabel II

44

The results of the elections were decided in advance to rotate power between the liberal and conservative parties. Powerful landowners and politicians forced the people to vote for who they said.

He was born in 1843 and died in 1920. He is considered to be one of the great Spanish writers. One of his most famous works, *The Episodios Nacionales*, is a set of historical novels that covers almost 100 years of history in Spain.

- Play *Back to the board*. One pupil stands in front of the class with their back to the board, another pupil writes a person or event from the lesson on the board. The pupil with his/her back to the board has to ask five questions to try and guess who or what they are.

The **Generation of '98** was a group of writers and intellectuals who wrote critically about Spain's politics. Members included Pío Baroja, Miguel de Unamuno and Antonio Machado.

Benito Pérez Galdós was another influential writer from this time. Find out more about him.

Learn more

- In the computer lab or at home, have pupils search for basic information on another writer of the *Generation of '98* and their works. They can make a fact file and present it to the class.

Crisis of '98: A short war with the United States ended with Spain losing its last overseas territories: Cuba, Puerto Rico and the Philippines. This 'end of an Empire' created many negative feelings about Spain within its own citizens.

Groups left out of the *turno pacífico* system grew stronger, like Catalan and Basque regionalists, as well as working-class parties.

Tip

Although the *turno pacifico* created stability it was corrupt and unfair. Make a *pros* and *cons* list on the board. Pros: *stability; economic growth*. Cons: *outside groups are not represented; people don't have power to make changes.* etc. Debate whether or not it's a good idea for a country to use such a system.

1902–1931

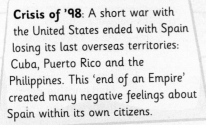

As more and more people saw this system as corrupt and damaging, confidence in the government fell and violent protests broke out. A **military coup** lead by **Miguel Primo de Rivera** succeeded. Alfonso XIII supported Primo de Rivera's **dictatorship** for seven years.

 **STAGE 1**

- Choose one important person from the Restoration and create a digital exhibit about them. It could be a profile with an image of the person and a short text about why they were important.
- Use different fonts and colourful backgrounds. Save your project on your computer to use later.

Name: .....
Born: .....
Died: .....
Role in the Restoration: .....
Interesting facts: .....

45

Pupils complete this stage at home in their notebooks so you can check it later. Remind them to make their slide interesting but not too distracting.

For the next lesson … one piece of paper or index card for each pupil with one word written on it from the following list: 60% of the cards: *working class, factory worker, farm worker*; 30% of the cards: *middle class, doctor, small business owner*; 10% of the cards: *upper class, nobility, factory owners*

Objective

Pupils will learn what happens in a modernising society.

Key vocabulary

agriculture, bourgeoisie, capitalist classes, industrial, modernisation, labour movement, nobility, middle class, rural, unions, upper class, urban, working class

Warm up

- Play *Pictionary* with some of the key vocabulary from the unit.

Main concepts

- Give each pupil a card with a member of the capitalist class written on it. Tell them they can't show anyone. Explain to pupils that you want them to get in groups according to class. They can walk around and explain who they are, but they must not say what is on the card. When they find someone of the same class they stay together and search for more people in their class.

Learn more

- Ask pupils to imagine spending a day as a person in one of the capitalist classes during the Restoration. Have them write a journal entry describing a day in their life. They should use the drawing, documentary and written descriptions for help.

Modernisation is when a society moves away from traditional agriculture in rural areas to an industrial, urban life.

The first built in Spain was actually in Cuba when it was a Spanish territory. The first on mainland Spain was from Barcelona to Mataró 10 years later in 1848.

WHAT IS MODERNISATION?

Discover... the changes that take place when a society modernises.

The Restoration was a time of **modernisation** in Spain. Modernisation is when a society moves away from traditional agriculture in rural areas to an industrial, urban life.

In a modern society …

society is organised in capitalist classes.

Railways were a major factor in modernisation. Where was the first one in Spain?

the population moves from rural to urban areas.

more people start to work in factories than on farms and in workshops.

Find another gear hidden in the unit!

Upper class: mainly made up of nobility, but a new group of rich factory owners and bankers were able to join with the money they made from their successful businesses. This group was called the *bourgeoisie*.

Middle class: they were less wealthy than the upper class. They were professionals, such as lawyers, doctors and small business owners.

Working class: factory workers in cities joined agricultural workers as the biggest class in modern society. They worked long hours for very low wages.

Labour movement: The working class grouped together and formed unions to protect themselves and improve working conditions.

Listen to a report on the Industrial Revolution in Spain. Write down the places you hear and what they produced.

46

B1 Preliminary for Schools **Listening Part 3.**

Cataluña: textiles

País Vasco and Cantabria: iron and steel

Asturias: coal

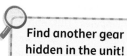

Gear on page 52

Yes, it lasted much longer and achieved many social and political reforms. However, it was in power when the Civil War broke out.

Because it had supported the dictatorship of Primo de Rivera.

WAS THE SECOND REPUBLIC MORE SUCCESSFUL THAN THE FIRST?

People became increasingly unhappy with the dictatorship. Alfonso XIII called for elections to try and win back their trust, but it was too late. The people voted for a republic and Alfonso XIII left Spain. On 14 April 1931, Spain **became a republic** again.

In the first years of the **Second Republic**, the government created a new constitution and introduced social reforms. It carried out:

- education reforms, including building thousands of new schools and removing religion as a mandatory subject.

- land reforms that gave farm workers the opportunity to purchase land for themselves.

- labour reforms to improve the conditions and lives of workers.

Not everyone agreed with the new social reforms. It was a time of violence and extreme actions by all political groups. It started Spain on the path towards civil war.

On 17 and 18 July 1936, a **military uprising** against the Republic was led by a group of generals including **Francisco Franco**. The coup was not successful everywhere, leaving the country divided.

Discover...
the reforms and changes made during the Second Republic.

Why do you think the people mistrusted the monarchy?

The Constitution of 1931:

- guaranteed freedom of expression.

- gave the right to vote to both men and women for the first time!

- separated the Church from the government and took away its privileges.

What else did the Constitution say?

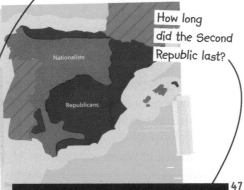

How long did the Second Republic last?

47

Example answers: It made divorce legal, granted freedom of religion, gave the right to vote to men and women, separated the church from the government.

It lasted from 1931–1939 when the Republicans lost the war. However, from 1936–1939 it only existed in parts of the country which were under Republican control.

For next lesson ... image of the *Guernica* by Picasso to show the pupils.

Objective

Pupils will learn about the actions and effects of the Second Republic.

Key vocabulary

constitution, education reforms, elections, land reforms, mandatory, social reform, vote

Warm up

- Write the word *Republic* on the board and ask pupils what they remember about it? When was the first one in Spain?

Main concepts

- Have pupils summarise the Second Republic in their notebooks: when it was, its reforms and its problems. Show different ways to summarise material, for example: bullet points, making a table, using a highlighter, using different colours to write, etc. Share which techniques work for you and ask the class which ones they use.

Learn more

- Explain that the Second Republic was and still is a polarising subject for many people. In pairs, have the pupils discuss why it made some groups upset and other groups excited. Could there have been a compromise between the groups?

Objective

Pupils will study the reasons for the Nationalist victory in the Civil War.

Key vocabulary

aid, generals, military, militia, Nationalist, Republicans, unity

Warm up

- Write the dates *1898, 1902, 1923, 1931, 1936* on the board. Pupils look back through the unit and say what happened during those years.

Main concepts

- Have pupils read out a factor from during the war. For example; *were mainly untrained militia; received support from Italy.* Their partner decides if the statements refer to the *Republicans* or *Nationalists*.

- Pupils make two columns in their notebooks: *Why the Nationalists won* and *Why the Republicans lost.* Using the information on the page, pupils write three reasons in each column.

Learn more

- Show pupils the image of the painting *Guernica* by Pablo Picasso. Discuss how it makes pupils feel, what pupils see and why they think Picasso chose to use the images and colours that feature in the painting.

Almost three years of war which devastated Spain and its population.

A group of soldiers made up of civilians with little or no training.

It slows modernisation by destroying roads, railways and factories. It also disrupts social progress like education and healthcare.

WHAT HAPPENED NEXT?

Discover...
how the Nationalists won the Civil War.

Spain was divided into two sides: the **Nationalists** who supported Francisco Franco and the **Republicans** who supported the Second Republic. The war for control began.

After about two years of fighting, the Nationalists had occupied most of the country. The war ended on 1 April 1939 when the Nationalists took control of Madrid and Barcelona. The Spanish Civil War resulted in hundreds of thousands of deaths, as well as the destruction of large parts of Spain.

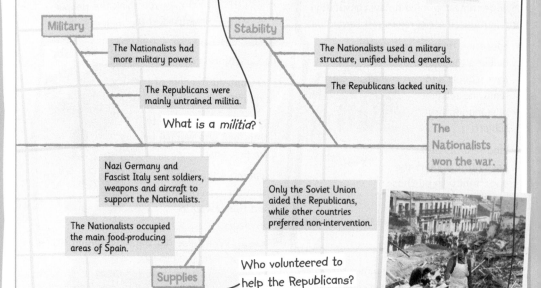

Military

The Nationalists had more military power.

The Republicans were mainly untrained militia.

What is a militia?

Stability

The Nationalists used a military structure, unified behind generals.

The Republicans lacked unity.

The Nationalists won the war.

Nazi Germany and Fascist Italy sent soldiers, weapons and aircraft to support the Nationalists.

Only the Soviet Union aided the Republicans, while other countries preferred non-intervention.

The Nationalists occupied the main food-producing areas of Spain.

Supplies

Who volunteered to help the Republicans?

How do think a war affects the modernisation of a country?

Explore   STAGE 2

- Act as an online archaeologist and 'dig up' a unique artefact, like a poster, piece of equipment or uniform from the civil war for your museum. Create a digital display.
- What is it? Where and how was it found? Add the information to your project.

48

Have pupils research at home and remind them of their search techniques from Unit 3. Encourage them to try and find something that tells a story and something that other pupils won't have. Ask them to write a description of the item so you can check their work.

Groups of people from other countries called the International Brigades.

For next lesson ... three propaganda images, three adverts, poster paper, craft materials

You need to choose colours and images that capture people's attention and represent what you want to say. Posters also need a slogan that communicates your message and that people can remember. They are usually short and written in the imperative tense. The poster should also be designed to consider the tastes and interests of the people you want to reach.

HOW DO YOU MAKE A PERSUASIVE POSTER?

Background: Posters and paintings have long been used to influence how people think or feel about certain ideas. These are often political ideas, but the techniques are also used in adverts to convince you to buy certain things.

Materials: poster paper, paints, pens, scissors, glue, craft materials

Task: Design a persuasive poster to convince teachers that homework or tests are a bad thing.

Step 1: Find three examples of propaganda posters and three adverts.

Step 2: Copy the table and answer the questions about the propaganda and adverts.

Why was it created?	Who was it made for?	What images and colours were used?	Do you think it achieves its goal?

Step 3: Choose your materials. Brainstorm ideas using the information in your table.

Step 4: Design your poster. Remember to design your poster for the specific audience: teachers.

Find Out more...

Discover... how images, colours and history are used to influence people's decisions.

EAT YOUR GREENS!

Slurpy

ICE COLD

Slurpy

NO MORE TESTS!

WE NEED A REST

49

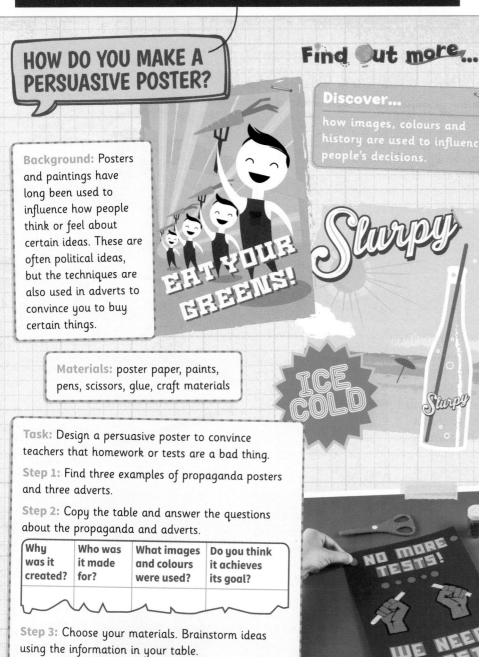

Objective

Pupils will explore how people are influenced by images, symbols and colours.

Key vocabulary

adverts, convince, influence, propaganda

Warm up

- Draw common symbols on the board or show images online. For example, skull and crossbones, a green circle, a stickman with a cloud over him, etc. Have pupils say what they think each symbol means.

Main concepts

- Show pupils the images and adverts you have brought to class and give them time to discuss answers to Step 2 in small groups. When they have completed the table, have them brainstorm and create their poster individually or in groups.

Learn more

- Pupils write a brief presentation explaining why their poster is the most convincing. They should explain what images and colours they used and why they chose them. After each poster has been explained, have pupils vote on which one they think is the most convincing.

UNIT 4
PAGES 50–51

Objective

Pupils will learn about life in Spain after the Civil War.

Key language

absolute power, autarky, censor, civil liberties, dictatorship, economic crisis, emigrate, illegal, prosper, rationing, repress, restricted

Warm up

- Draw a triple Venn diagram on the board and add the labels: *monarchy; dictatorship; republic.* As a class, brainstorm elements of the government types to complete the diagram. For example: *May contain a constitution.* (R, M); *Can have an absolute ruler.* (M, D); *Doesn't need a king or queen.* (D, R); *Was a style of government in Spain.* (M, R, D).

Main concepts

- Draw a fishbone chart like the one on page 48. Explain that this type of chart shows multiple causes creating one effect. In the head of the chart write, *Life in Spain post war.* Have pupils copy the chart and use the information from pages 50–51 to complete it in their notebooks.

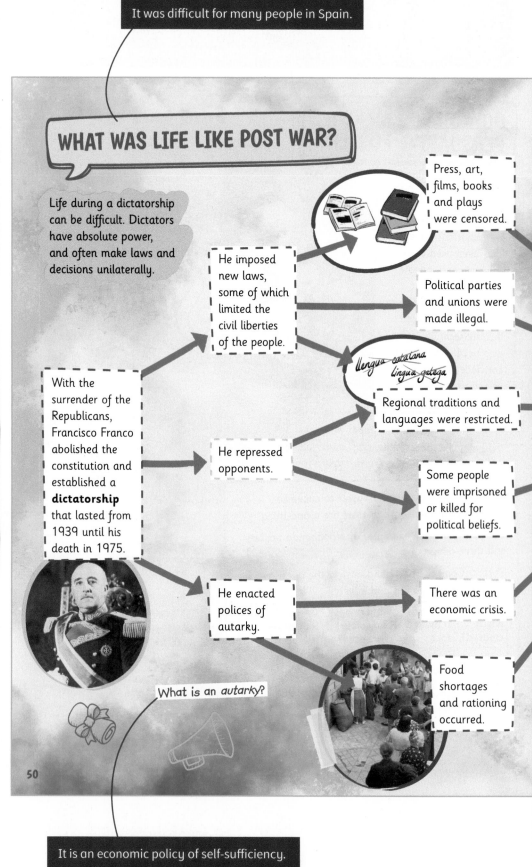

It was difficult for many people in Spain.

WHAT WAS LIFE LIKE POST WAR?

Life during a dictatorship can be difficult. Dictators have absolute power, and often make laws and decisions unilaterally.

With the surrender of the Republicans, Francisco Franco abolished the constitution and established a **dictatorship** that lasted from 1939 until his death in 1975.

He imposed new laws, some of which limited the civil liberties of the people.

Press, art, films, books and plays were censored.

Political parties and unions were made illegal.

Regional traditions and languages were restricted.

He repressed opponents.

Some people were imprisoned or killed for political beliefs.

He enacted polices of autarky.

There was an economic crisis.

What is an *autarky?*

Food shortages and rationing occurred.

It is an economic policy of self-sufficiency. A country produces everything it uses without trading with any others.

50

64

The government can hide anything bad about them or spread false information about political opponents.

To prevent ideas circulating in society that they believe are too sexual, blasphemous or politically subversive. They fear that if people are exposed to freedoms and new ideas expressed in the arts, people will start to question their rulers and eventually rebel.

Learn more

- Ask pupils to imagine that they are living in post-war Spain. Encourage them to write a journal entry describing the day in the life of a child. Elicit better descriptions by asking; *Is there a lot of food? Can you read any book you want? Can you have a celebration in your village? Is there work for your family?*

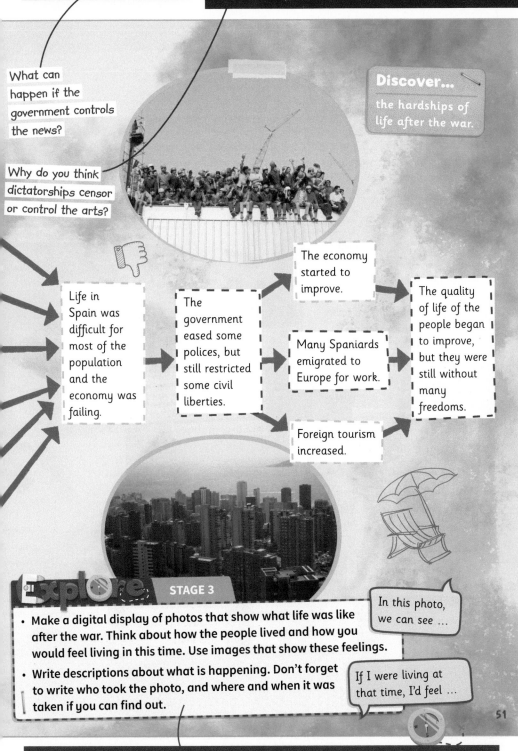

What can happen if the government controls the news?

Why do you think dictatorships censor or control the arts?

Discover...
the hardships of life after the war.

Life in Spain was difficult for most of the population and the economy was failing.

The government eased some polices, but still restricted some civil liberties.

The economy started to improve.

Many Spaniards emigrated to Europe for work.

Foreign tourism increased.

The quality of life of the people began to improve, but they were still without many freedoms.

STAGE 3

Explore

- Make a digital display of photos that show what life was like after the war. Think about how the people lived and how you would feel living in this time. Use images that show these feelings.
- Write descriptions about what is happening. Don't forget to write who took the photo, and where and when it was taken if you can find out.

In this photo, we can see ...

If I were living at that time, I'd feel ...

51

Pupils may need extra guidance to find the photos they want to show. Tell them they should search for photos of ordinary people in Spain going about their daily life. To achieve this, have them search for specific years and decades. Various news outlets have made photo albums of life in Spain after the war.

Tip

To make a more engaging lesson, explain that a lot of pop music was censored at the time. Songs like *Good Vibrations* by the Beach Boys and *Imagine* by John Lennon weren't allowed in Spain. Listen to the lyrics and see if the pupils can find why they would be censored. Ask if they think any music they listen to now would have been banned.

Objective

Pupils will learn the important dates leading up to and during democratic Spain.

Key vocabulary

appoint, democratic, elections, Prime Minister, referendum, reform, strike, transition

Warm up

- Write *Democracy*, *Dictatorship*, *Constitutional Monarchy*, *Absolute Monarchy*, *Republic* on the board. Have pupils describe each in their own words.

Main concepts

- Have pupils make a recipe for democracy. In groups, pupils use their own ideas as well as ideas from the unit to write all the 'ingredients' that are needed to make a democracy. Show them words such as *a dash* or *a pinch* for elements that are less important and *grams* and *kilos* for the more important issues. For example, *one kilo of free elections*, *800 grams of free speech*, *a dash of duties*, etc. When they are happy with their recipe, pupils can add pictures and symbols and display it in the school.

Years of turmoil, instability, different types of government and war left a country ready for democracy and a constitution.

Adolfo Suárez, Leopoldo Calvo-Sotelo, Felipe González, José María Aznar, José Luis Rodríguez Zapatero, Mariano Rajoy, Pedro Sánchez

HOW DID WE GET HERE?

Discover... the footsteps our society took to democracy and beyond.

With the death of Franco, the leaders and the people of Spain made a choice. After centuries of wars, uprisings and instability, they chose to peacefully transition to democracy.

Who won the election? List the names of all the Prime Ministers up to the present day.

Franco appointed Prince Juan Carlos to replace him. When Franco died in November 1975, **King Juan Carlos I** began the process to transition Spain into a democracy.

Juan Carlos I is the great, great-grandson of Isabel II. Who are his great-grandfather and grandfather?

In June 1977, the first democratic elections were held in Spain in 40 years.

In 1976, **Adolfo Suárez** was appointed as Prime Minister by the king. He led the reform of new political laws that:

legalised political parties and trade unions.

gave workers the right to strike.

released political prisoners.

opened the door to free elections.

NO! NO! NO! NO!

52

Alfonso XII and Alfonso XIII

Here's the hidden object!

Extra Activity, Page 93:
Have the class create a time capsule about their lives for future generations to open and study.

Learn more

- Write a thank you letter to the people who fought for and chose to create a democracy in Spain. Tell pupils to mention what freedoms they enjoy, thank them for their choice and hard work and tell them that they will continue to stand up for democracy.

On 6 December 1978, the citizens of Spain voted in favour of the **Constitution** through a referendum. It established Spain as a democracy by creating a constitutional monarchy and guaranteeing Spanish citizens' rights, like equality, freedom of expression and voting.

Is this the same constitution we use today?

After the election, the elected political parties created a new constitution.

Constitución Española

1982: Spain joined the North Atlantic Treaty Organization (NATO).

1986: Spain entered the EEC, which later became the European Union.

2002: Spain officially entered the Eurozone, replacing the peseta with the euro as its currency.

Today, pupils read about democracy in Spain!

Tip

Draw a large timeline on the board starting in 1800 to today. Have pupils look back over units 3 and 4 and write the type of government that ruled and for how long.

1808–1812 Absolute Monarchy; 1812–1814 Constitutional Monarchy; 1814–1820 AM; 1820–23 CM; 1823–33 AM; 1833–73 CM; 1874 Republic; 1875–1923 CM; 1923–1930 Dictatorship; 1931–1939 Republic; 1939–1975 Dictatorship; 1975–today Democracy, Parliamentary Monarchy

Explore — STAGE 4

- We can find out about recent events in history from videos and first-hand accounts. Find a person you know who lived through an important event in Spain's transition to democracy. Record an interview with them about their experience.
- If the interview is in Spanish, provide a translation for non-Spanish speakers.

How did you feel?

Were you nervous or excited?

What were other people doing?

53

In class, brainstorm possible people to interview and questions to ask. Pupils do the interview at home. Remind them that they cannot record anyone without that person's permission. Tell them they can conduct the interview in Spanish, but they will need to provide a translation in English.

Language Review answers

1 b She can't be Isabel II.

  c They must be the working class.

  d He could be Juan Carlos I.

  e It could be the Constitution of 1931.

  f He must be Antonio Cánovas del Castillo.

2 b slowed, had destroyed

  c had been, started

  d ruled, had been

  e didn't trust, had supported

3 Pupils' own answers

> This activity gives pupils practice of *B1 Preliminary for Schools* Speaking Part 3

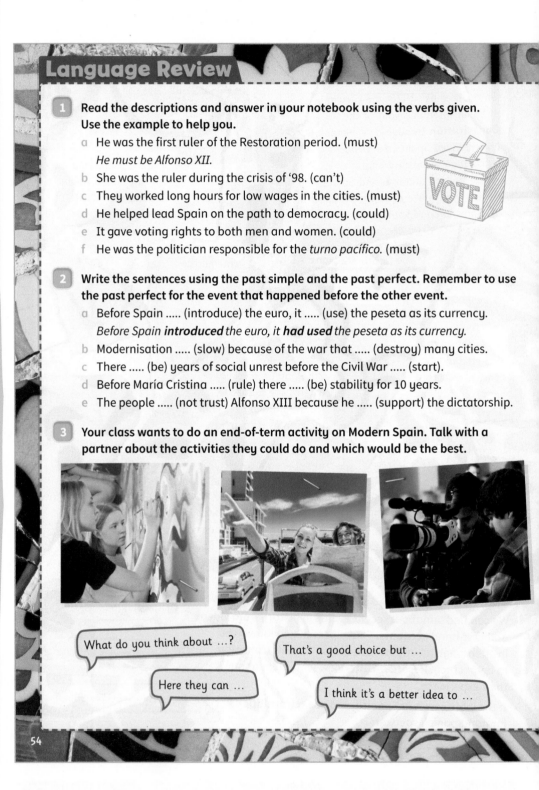

Language Review

1 Read the descriptions and answer in your notebook using the verbs given. Use the example to help you.

  a He was the first ruler of the Restoration period. (must)
    He must be Alfonso XII.

  b She was the ruler during the crisis of '98. (can't)

  c They worked long hours for low wages in the cities. (must)

  d He helped lead Spain on the path to democracy. (could)

  e It gave voting rights to both men and women. (could)

  f He was the politician responsible for the *turno pacífico*. (must)

2 Write the sentences using the past simple and the past perfect. Remember to use the past perfect for the event that happened before the other event.

  a Before Spain ..... (introduce) the euro, it ..... (use) the peseta as its currency.
    *Before Spain **introduced** the euro, it **had used** the peseta as its currency.*

  b Modernisation ..... (slow) because of the war that ..... (destroy) many cities.

  c There ..... (be) years of social unrest before the Civil War ..... (start).

  d Before María Cristina ..... (rule) there ..... (be) stability for 10 years.

  e The people ..... (not trust) Alfonso XIII because he ..... (support) the dictatorship.

3 Your class wants to do an end-of-term activity on Modern Spain. Talk with a partner about the activities they could do and which would be the best.

What do you think about ...?

That's a good choice but ...

Here they can ...

I think it's a better idea to ...

54

Encourage pupils to revise the unit content using the techniques on page 85.

Content Review

Content Review answers

1 1875–1931: The Restoration - Alfonso XII; María Cristina; Alfonso XIII.

1931–1936: The Second Republic

1936–1939: The Civil War

1939–1975: Franco's Dictatorship - Francisco Franco

1975–Today: Democratic Spain - Adolfo Suárez; Leopoldo Calvo-Sotelo; Felipe González; José María Aznar; José Luis Rodríguez Zapatero; Mariano Rajoy; Pedro Sánchez

2 a The Second Republic

b The Restoration

c Franco's dictatorship

d The Restoration

e Democratic Spain

f The Second Republic

g Democratic Spain

1 Copy the timeline and label the time periods. Add the leaders of Spain during each period.

Assessment link
For more Unit 4 activities go to page 84.

Democratic Spain   Franco's dictatorship   The Civil War
The Restoration   The Second Republic

1875-1931	1931-1936	1936-1939	1939-1975	1975-today

2 Match the events a–g to the periods of time from Activity 1.

a Women gained the right to vote for the first time.
b A system of false elections created stability.
c Spain had a system called autarky.
d This was a period of modernisation in Spain.
e Spain joined the European Union.
f A military uprising led to a civil war.
g The first democratic elections in 40 years were held.

 **Explore** — **FINALE**

- Now you can combine all your digital exhibits on a program for making presentations. This is your digital museum.
- Give it a name because you are going to take your class on a tour!
- Prepare a tour with an opening statement welcoming everyone, a brief description of each exhibit and a closing statement that thanks everyone for their visit. You can make notecards to help you remember what to say.

This exhibit shows …

Did you know that … ?

Please, no flash photography!

55

Give pupils a few days to make the presentation and practise their speech at home. Set a time limit for the tour and explain to pupils that they mustn't go over. To do this, encourage pupils to practise at home in front of the mirror and their families. Setting a time limit helps save time and teaches pupils about preparation.

Think about it answers

1 It was from 1875–1931. The rulers were Alfonso XII, María Cristina (regent) and Alfonso XIII.

2 Spain lost its last overseas territories. It created a feeling of negativity in the Spanish people.

3 A system of electoral manipulation that rotated power between the liberal and conservative parties.

4 People move from rural areas into the big cities.

5 It built and reformed schools, gave the right to vote to men and women and made land available for farm workers to purchase.

6 It started in July 1936 and ended on 1 April 1939.

7 The Nationalists used a military structure unified behind generals and received aid and supplies from Germany and Italy.

8 There were food shortages, a failing economy and limited freedoms for the Spanish people.

9 Juan Carlos I

10 Example answers: Adolfo Suárez legalised political parties; First democratic elections held in 40 years; The Constitution of 1978 was approved on 6 December

---

Think harder answers

1 Pupils' own answers

2 The political stability and peace allowed modernisation to progress quickly.

3 Pupils' own answers

4 They felt that it had grown too powerful.

5 Example answer: The government and laws don't represent all the people of a country. A certain group can gain too much control.

6 Example answers: people can move up to the upper class without belonging to the nobility; new technology improves peoples lives such as better transportation; urban areas developed into the cities we live in today.

7 He was in Africa. The isolated location allowed his ideas to spread without much resistance.

8 Pupils' own answers

9 Carlos III—Carlos IV---Fernando VII—Isabel II—Alfonso XII—Alfonso XIII—Juan Carlos I—Felipe VI

10 Pupils' own answers

UNIT 4 TRACKLIST

5

OUR RIGHTS, OUR COUNTRY, OUR CONSTITUTION

Learning objectives

By the end of this unit, pupils will have achieved a greater understanding of the following concepts:

- the main democratic ideals of the Constitution
- the importance of the Constitution to the function and organisation of the Spanish government
- the division of state powers
- the main institutions of the Spanish government

Competences

This unit covers the following competences:

- Linguistic competence
- Social and civic competences
- Digital competence
- Learning to learn
- Initiative and entrepreneurship

Key vocabulary

Constitution: assistance, democracy, democratic, duties, duty, education, freedom, healthcare, justice, limits, negotiating, rights, speaker, social, unanimous, voting

Government: branch of government, Central Government, Congress, Constitutional Court, Court of Law, Executive branch, institution, Judicial branch, Legislative branch, Parliament, parliamentary monarchy, political background, Senate, taxes, Tribunals

People: councillors, deputy, head of state, judge, magistrate, mayor, ministers, prime minister, senator

Country: autonomous communities, municipalities, provinces, provincial council, self-governing, Statute of Autonomy, town council

Cambridge English Qualifications practice

You will find **B1 Preliminary for Schools** activity types in the following exercises:
Pupil's Book, Page 63 – Listening Part 3
Pupil's Book, Page 66, Activity 3 – Writing Part 2
Activity Book, Page 30, Activity 9 – Reading Part 3

Throughout this unit, you will find the following **B1 Preliminary for Schools** vocabulary: arrange, background, belong, duty, education, expert, interpret, judge, limit, member, social, voice

Materials needed for *Find out more*

- large sticky notes
- poster board
- art materials

Materials needed for other activities

- poster board
- art materials
- index cards
- sticky tape
- one blank map of the provinces of Spain per group of four
- one map of the provinces of Spain labelled

Explore

The *Explore* project encourages pupils to think about how it must have felt to transition into democracy. They will make a news broadcast from 1977 explaining the Constitution with visual aids. The different *Explore* stages practise the following skills:

- displaying information to teach important points
- making games to study
- writing scripts
- recording and editing a video

Digital Lab 6 Social Science

Interactive activities

Flashcards

Song: *It's my right!*

Video documentary: *A brief guide to democracy*

Objective

Pupils will learn to think about the Constitution and how it affects them.

Key vocabulary

constitution, duties, freedom, political background, protection, rights

Warm up

- Write on the board: *What do we need for a democracy?* Have pupils discuss with a partner what they think is needed to have a democracy. Pupils write their best answers on the board. When all answers are written, ask: *How do we protect these things?* (With a constitution).

Main concepts

- Explain that citizens have freedom and duties in the Constitution and that the government has duties too. Pupils look at the photos and decide if it is a personal duty, a freedom or a governmental duty.

- Have a pupil act out a freedom or duty while the class tries to guess.

(Photos 1, 2, 6) The right to protest, freedom of expression and voting rights guarantee that our voices are heard, and the government reflects our interests.

(Photo 3) Social health care protects our health.

5 OUR RIGHTS, OUR COUNTRY, OUR CONSTITUTION

Look and discuss...

What is happening in each photo?

In 1977, a newly-elected parliament had to create a constitution. They chose seven members from different political backgrounds to write it. On 31 October 1978 it was approved by the parliament, and on 6 December 1978 by the people.

In this photo people are …

This shows …

1 a protest; 2 a political rally/conference; 3 someone receiving medical care; 4 children attending school; 5 travelling; 6 voting; 7 taking care of the environment

56

(Photo 4) Free education protects equality by giving all children a chance to learn.

(Photo 5) The freedom to travel protects equality and our right to choose where we live.

(Photo 7) The duty to take care of the environment protects our future.

Learn more

- Ask pupils to imagine what life would be like today without a constitution and create a short role-play. *What could happen? How would life be different?*

Song
This song focuses on the rights and freedoms granted by the Constitution. It can be used on pages 58–59.

Documentary
The documentary lets pupils explore the process of voting, from attending speeches, discussing issues with friends and family to making a decision and casting a vote. It can be used on pages 56–57 and 62–63.

Tip

Play the documentary and have pupils find all the freedoms and rights they see in the video that are also pictured in the lesson and try to figure out any more they haven't learned yet.

How do the actions in the photos protect you?

S ng
It's my right!

What happens on 6 December every year?

DOCUMENTARY
A brief guide to democracy

Explore

Travel back in time to 1977. The Spanish people have just got a lot of new rights, rules and systems, but they need a team of experts to help explain it all. You will:

- explain the new rights and systems to the Spanish people.
- create visual aids to help them understand.
- build a game to help pupils learn.
- record a news report for the class to watch.

57

Explain that pupils will make a news broadcast from 1977. Brainstorm what elements are typically present during news broadcasts. Tell them to watch a few news programmes to better understand. Tell pupils that they will need to dress like news anchors from 1977. Have them ask family members for advice and search for photos online.

It's a bank holiday to celebrate the Constitution. Events are held all over Spain to celebrate this important moment in our history.

For next lesson … poster board and art materials

Objective

Pupils will be able to identify the basic principles guaranteed by the Constitution and its role in the function of the government.

Key vocabulary

assistance, democracy, democratic, duty, education, freedom, healthcare, justice, right, social, taxes

Warm up

- Tell pupils to look at the drawings of the Constitution wearing hats. Ask: *What jobs is it doing?* Elicit *chef*, *superhero* and *constructor*. In pairs, pupils write down verbs that can be used for each job and circle which words also apply to a constitution: *cook, make, mix, protect, defend, fight, design, build, plan*

Main concepts

- Have pupils make a table with three columns: *What the Constitution does for me*; *What the government must do*; *What I must do*. Pupils write three ideas in each column. They share their ideas with their partner and add any answers they don't have.

- Play *Constitutional or Unconstitutional*. Pupils make a sentence describing a scenario. For example; *Peaceful protesters arrested*; *I can practise whichever religion I like*. The other pupils then say if the action is *Constitutional* or *Unconstitutional*.

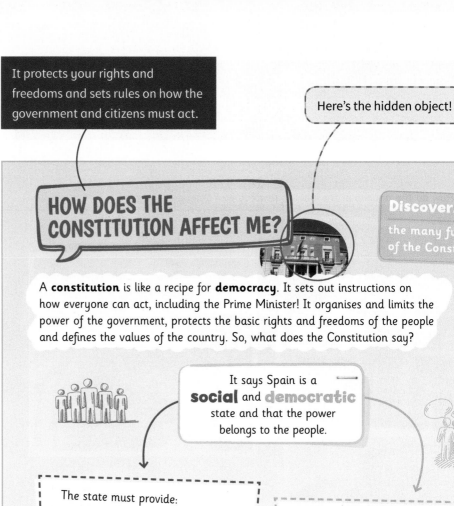

It protects your rights and freedoms and sets rules on how the government and citizens must act.

Here's the hidden object!

HOW DOES THE CONSTITUTION AFFECT ME?

Discover... the many functions of the Constitution.

A **constitution** is like a recipe for **democracy**. It sets out instructions on how everyone can act, including the Prime Minister! It organises and limits the power of the government, protects the basic rights and freedoms of the people and defines the values of the country. So, what does the Constitution say?

It says Spain is a **social** and **democratic** state and that the power belongs to the people.

The state must provide:
- basic education
- healthcare
- assistance for people without work
- opportunities for decent housing

Elections are held to decide members of the government every four years.

Look back...

How was life different under a dictator or absolute monarch than with the Constitution?

58

With the Constitution the government represents the will and ideas of the people because they have the right to vote, protest and participate in government.

Autonomous communities can have their own official languages, symbols and flags along with Castilian and the flag of Spain. It protects all cultures and traditions of Spain.

Extra Activity, Page 94:

Pupils use their freedom of expression to create a class newspaper.

Learn more

- Listen to the song, *It's my Right!* Have pupils point to the section in the lesson where each right can be found. After listening a few times, have pupils write their own verses for the song in pairs. Ask for volunteers to perform their rights rap to the rest of the class.

It explains the individual rights, freedoms and duties of the people:

Rights

- Right to freedom, equality and justice
- Freedom of speech and expression
- Freedom of religion
- Right to strike and protest peacefully
- Freedom to travel and choose where to live
- Right to vote for all citizens 18 years and older

Duties

- Respect the law
- Respect the rights of others
- Pay taxes
- Take care of the environment

It creates a parliamentary monarchy and divides up power throughout the government, but gives the most power to the people.

Tip

To help pupils review the lesson, have them think of any other jobs or hats that could represent the role of the Constitution in society. They should write three to five ideas in their notebooks. For example: *The Constitution is like an engineer because it designs and builds our government.*

Find out what the Constitution says about languages and flags.

How does the Constitution give the power to the people?

STAGE 1

- Create your news team of reporters and experts. Together, make a poster with the most important rights and duties outlined in the Constitution.
- Add drawings or pictures to help explain the ideas. Remember to make it interesting and easy to understand.
- Write out a short script, roughly a minute long, explaining your poster.

The most important rights / duties in the Constitution are ...

It is the most important right / duty because it gives us ...

59

Put pupils into groups of four. Give them time in class to make the poster and write out the script.

The people control who is in the government and have the freedom of expression and the right to protest. The power of the Senators, Deputies and Prime Minister comes from the people.

For next lesson ... large sticky notes, poster board, art materials

Objective

Pupils will find out more about the Constitution by creating their own and learning about voting and negotiating.

Key vocabulary

limits, speaker, negotiating, unanimous, voting

Warm up

- Ask pupils: *What is the perfect classroom?* Have them shout out their answers. Then, say in a stern voice: *That's enough! You don't make the rules, I do.* Explain that is what life is like without a constitution. Tell pupils that if they had a class constitution, maybe their voice could be heard.

Main concepts

- Help pupils begin by having them vote for a speaker of the class. Set time limits to keep the activity on task. However, this activity should be run as much as possible by the pupils and the speaker of the class with very little teacher involvement.

Learn more

- Pupils create an official document with all the new rights and duties listed and the signatures of the class. Pupils also create posters displaying individual rights and duties with drawings and symbols.

Through negotiations and voting.

HOW DO YOU MAKE A CONSTITUTION?

Find Out more...

Discover... the process of voting and negotiating.

Background: In a country without a constitution, the people have nothing to protect their rights and have no control or voice in what happens. The government or even one person can make all the decisions without limits. Does that sound familiar? That changes today, with a class constitution!

Materials: large sticky notes, posters, markers

Task: Write a class constitution.

- Elect a pupil to be the speaker of the class. They lead, control and count the votes.

- In groups, brainstorm what pupils and teachers need in a classroom.

- Arrange your ideas to make one law for each category:

  Write them out on four sticky notes and stick them to the board.

- Read and vote on each idea. If more than half of the class votes for it, it can stay.

- It's time for a final vote. The vote must be unanimous. If not, discuss, debate and vote until everyone agrees.

- Make posters to display your constitution.

Rights of Pupils

Rights of Teachers

Duties of Pupils

Duties of Teachers

Who votes for idea ... ?

Everyone in favour say *Yes* and everyone against say *No*.

We could add ...

I think we need ...

60

78

Control is divided up among the different branches of the State, but all powers come from the Spanish people.

If a person has multiple jobs in the government, they will have too much power and the system of division of power will fail. Example jobs; President, Senator, Judge.

WHO'S IN CONTROL?

The Constitution set up a **parliamentary monarchy**. This divided the power of the state into three different branches. This way no person or group has all the power.

Executive branch. This branch decides the political and economic direction of the government. It proposes the budget to be voted on. It enforces the law.

Discover...
how power is divided in the state.

The Constitutional Court.
An institution that makes sure no person, law or government violates the Constitution. It is made up of 12 magistrates who are experts in law.

Executive branch

Judicial branch

Legislative branch

Judicial branch. It can interpret laws, decide punishments and settle disagreements over legal matters.

Legislative branch. Its main function is to make and approve laws. It also approves the budget and watches over the Executive branch to make sure they are governing properly.

No person can have a job in different branches at the same time. Why is this important? What are some of the jobs?

Explore   STAGE 2

- On this page a pie chart is used to show the division of powers. With your group make a flowchart or think of another idea to show how the power of the state divides into branches and what they do.
- Draw your ideas in your notebook.

61

Give pupils time in class to brainstorm ideas and then draw and label one chart or diagram. Tell them that they will need to use this drawing again so to leave some space and keep it safe.

For next lesson ... poster board, art materials, index cards, tape

Objective

Pupils will examine how the Constitution divides the power of the government and the functions of the institutions of Spain.

Key vocabulary

branch of government, Constitutional Court, Executive, Judicial, Legislative, parliamentary monarchy

Warm up

- Ask: *What powers does the government have?* Elicit, *make laws, enforce laws, decide punishments, plan budgets, spend money* and write them on the board.

Main concepts

- Using different colours for *Legislative, Executive* and *Judicial*, have pupils circle the powers from the Warm-up exercise with the colour of the branch that possesses it.

Learn more

- Play *Who said it?* Write the following sentences on the board: *We should spend one million euros on this.* (Executive); *Hey, that's against the Constitution.* (Constitutional Court). The class decides if the *Judicial, Legislative, Executive* or the *Constitutional Court* would say it. Pupils make more statements and play with a partner.

Objective

Pupils will study the institutions of Spain, their organisation and function.

Key vocabulary

Central Government, Congress, Court of Law, deputy, head of state, institution, judge, magistrate, ministers, Parliament, prime minister, Senate, senator, Tribunals

Warm up

- Give each pupil a card and have them write one of the following words on the card: *senator, deputy, king, queen, prime minister, minister, judge*. While the pupils work, write *Central Government, Senate, Congress of Deputies* and *Courts of Law* on the board. Have pupils place their cards where they believe the person works.

Main concepts

- Play *Who am I?* Take the cards from the Warm-up activity and shuffle them. Hand them out face down. Have pupils put sellotape on the back and tape it to their foreheads without looking. Pupils ask a partner *Yes* or *No* questions to work out who they are. For example: *Do I work in … ?; Have I got the power to … ?; Am I part of the … branch?*

An elected government official who works in the Senate to create and approve laws.

WHAT'S A SENATOR?

Discover... the structure of the main institutions of Spain.

The Constitution created **institutions** to control each branch. The members in each branch represent the people, the central government or the law.

Executive

The **Central Government** is the institution of this branch. The head of the branch is the **Prime Minister** (*Presidente del Gobierno*) who is elected by the Congress of Deputies and appointed by the King. The Prime Minister appoints **ministers** to control areas of the government like agriculture, defence or justice.

The king or queen is the **Head of State**. The Head of State cannot pass any laws but is a key representative of Spain in affairs with other countries.

Where does the Prime Minister live?

Find the Prime Minister's residence hidden in the unit!

Have you heard about any of these institutions on the news? Find out their official names in Spain.

62

The Palacio de Moncloa on page 58.

The Prime Minister lives in the Palacio de Moncloa.

Parliament: *Cortes Generales*

Senate: *Senado*

Congress of Deputies: *Congreso de los Diputados*

Central Government: *Gobierno*

The Legislative Branch.

Legislative

The institution of this branch is the **Parliament**. It is divided into two chambers: the **Senate** and the **Congress of Deputies**. There are 266 **senators** and 350 **deputies**. They are elected by the Spanish people every four years.

Which branch could be called the voice of the Spanish people?

Tip

Individually in the computer lab or together in class, use an online map to find the location of the main government buildings in Madrid. For example: *the Senate, Congress, Supreme Court, Constitutional Court, Palacio de la Moncloa*

Judicial

The **courts of law** and **tribunals** are made up of **judges** and **magistrates**. They are arranged in levels. The **Supreme Court** is the highest level and can change any decision made by a lower court.

🎧 Listen to a woman talking to a group of pupils about her job as a deputy in Congress. Write down three things she has to do today.

Explore — STAGE 3

- Add the name of the institutions and who works in each to your flowchart from Stage 2.
- When you are happy with your plan, make a larger version on a poster to use in your news report. Write a quick one-minute explanation.

... work in the ...

Its job is to ...

63

Give pupils time to complete their chart from the last stage and create a poster-sized version. They can finish the poster at home if needed.

B1 Preliminary for Schools Listening Part 3

Vote on a proposal; Speak in front of Congress; Have a meeting with a group of students about pollution in their neighbourhood.

For next lesson ... index cards; one map showing the provinces of Spain without labels for each group of four; one map showing the labelled provinces of Spain.

Objective

Pupils will study how the Constitution organises Spain and the name and location of its provinces.

Key vocabulary

autonomous communities,
councillors, mayor,
municipalities, provinces,
provincial council, self-governing,
Statute of Autonomy,
town council

Warm up

- Divide the class in two and give each group a piece of chalk. Tell them they must write all the autonomous communities of Spain on the board. The first group to finish wins. Each pupil can only write one name before passing the chalk to the next pupil.

Main concepts

- Place the labelled map of the provinces of Spain on your desk and hand out the blank maps of Spain to pupils in their groups of four. In their groups, pupils must write the names of all 50 provinces on their blank map. To do this, one pupil walks to the labelled map, returns and tells their group the name of a province and where it is. They cannot point, touch or write themselves. They walk back to the map for another name. After a minute, a new member of the groups goes. The first group to finish wins.

They are the communities, provinces and municipalities of Spain.

WHAT ARE ALL THOSE LINES ON THE MAP?

Discover...
how Spain is divided into smaller self-governing territories.

The Constitution organised Spain into **autonomous communities**, **provinces** and **municipalities**. It permits the autonomous communities to be **self-governing**. Each has its own name, boundaries, capital, flag and official languages, as well as its own set of laws that describe how each community will make decisions. It is called the **Statute of Autonomy**.

Municipalities are the smallest territories. Each has a **town council** with a **mayor** and **councillors** who are elected by the residents of the municipality. The council coordinates public services like street cleaning.

Municipalities group together to form a province. **Provinces** can have their own government called the **provincial council**. It coordinates services for the municipalities.

64

The Legislative branch makes and approves laws.

The Executive branch makes the political and economic decisions.

The Judicial branch interprets laws.

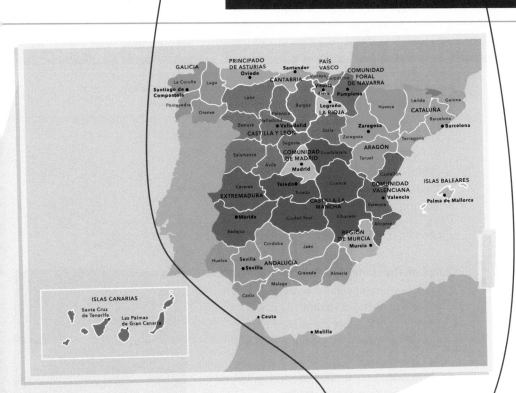

The **autonomous communities** have their own institutions to make decisions and pass laws. They are divided into three branches just like the national institutions:

- **Executive**: A president and councillors
- **Legislative**: A parliament elected by the people
- **Judicial**: Courts of the community

Do you remember the function of each branch?

Some provinces have the same name as the community. Why do you think that is?

 **STAGE 4**

- Create a memory game to help people remember the territories. Make two cards for each autonomous community: one with the name of the community and the other with the names of the provinces. Make one card for each autonomous city.

- Place them face down and try to match them. Now, write a script for an advertisement to sell your game. Remember to make it exciting and name a price in pesetas!

Do you have problems remembering ... ?

It's so much fun and only costs ... pesetas!

65

Language Review answers

1 Pupils' own answers. (Make sure the pupils are using reported speech as in the example.)

2 a too

b enough

c enough

d enough, too

3 Pupils' own answers

This activity gives pupils practice of *B1 Preliminary for Schools* Writing Part 2

Language Review

1 Interview a classmate about their feelings on the Constitution. In your notebook, write their answers in reported speech.

a What do you think are the most important freedoms or rights in the Constitution?
b How do you feel about the division of powers?
c Would you change anything about the Constitution?
d Add a question of your own.

She said that freedom of religion was the most important freedom.

2 Complete the sentences with *too* or *enough*.
a The government was ..... powerful so they wrote a constitution to limit its power.
b The idea got ..... votes to make it a law.
c The politician wasn't popular ..... to get elected.
d There wasn't ..... support for the law because the competition was ..... strong.

3 You see this notice in a magazine. Write your article in about 100 words.

**Articles wanted!
The Constitution**

*What is the most important part of the Constitution?
Is it the separation of powers, the rights and freedoms or both?
What could happen if there wasn't a constitution?
Tell us what you think!*

**Write an article answering these questions.
The best ones will be published in next month's issue.**

66

Encourage pupils to revise the unit content using the techniques on page 87

Content Review

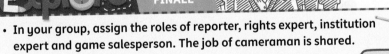

Assessment link

For more Unit 5 activities go to page 86.

1 Copy and complete the table.

Branch	Legislative	Executive	Judicial
Institutions			
Members			
Functions			

2 Read the descriptions and choose the correct word or phrase from the box.

> Constitutional Court   Head of State
> Statute of Autonomy   Province   Social State

a   This allows communities to create their own capitals, laws and institutions.
b   A government that provides basic needs like healthcare and education.
c   An institution that protects the Constitution.
d   A territory made up of municipalities.
e   The official representative of Spain, but with no real political power.

Explore

FINALE

- In your group, assign the roles of reporter, rights expert, institution expert and game salesperson. The job of cameraman is shared.
- Write out a beginning and ending for the reporter to say. Remember this is an exciting headline in history.
- Try to find clothing from that time period and make props like a microphone.
- Now it's time to film your news report. Lights, camera, action! Remember, if you practise a few times, you will be less nervous.

> Good evening, on this incredible day!

> Now, let's hear from an expert …

67

This can be done in class or at home. It can also be done live in front of the class without any cameras. Set a date for the performance or recording so pupils know when to bring in all the props. Give pupils time in class to practise and make props.

Content Review answers

1 Legislative

Institutions	Parliament, Senate, Congress of Deputies
Members	senators, deputies
Functions	Makes and approves laws; watches over Executive branch

Executive

Institutions	Central Government
Members	prime minister, ministers
Functions	Decides the political and economic direction of Spain

Judicial

Institutions	Courts, Tribunals
Members	judges, magistrates
Functions	Interprets laws and settles disagreements

2 a Statute of Autonomy

b Social State

c Constitutional Court

d Province

e Head of State

Think about it answers

1 It was approved by Parliament on 31 October 1978 and by the people on 6 December 1978.

2 It organises and divides the power of the government, gives instructions on how the government and citizens must act and guarantees and protects basic rights and freedoms for everyone.

3 It means the state provides education, health care and assistance to its people.

4 The right to strike, protest peacefully, vote and equality and justice. The Spanish people have freedom of speech and expression and freedom to travel and live wherever they choose.

5 The Legislative branch makes and approves laws. The Executive branch decides economic and political policy and the Judicial branch interprets laws and settles disputes.

6 To make sure no person or law violates the Constitution.

7 The Prime Minister.

8 In the Legislative branch.

9 The Supreme Court.

10 The autonomous communities are divided into provinces and the provinces are divided into municipalities.

Think harder answers

1 Power is divided into different branches of government so no one group has too much power. A constitution protects freedom of expression, press and the right to protest so all opinions can be heard. Voting rights are protected so that the government always reflects the ideas of the people.

2 It defines the basic values of the country.

3 The flag features three unequal horizontal stripes to make it unique. Its coat of arms shows shields of old Spanish kingdoms between the pillars of Hercules to honour Spain's history. A crown is set on the coat of arms for the monarchy.

4 It protects the languages and traditions of all the regions of Spain as a vital part of Spanish culture.

5 Pupils' own answers

6 Pupils' own answers

7 Pupils' own answers

8 Pupils' own answers

9 Pupils' own answers

10 Pupils' own answers

UNIT 5 TRACKLIST

6

THE EUROPEAN UNION

Learning objectives

By the end of this unit, pupils will have achieved a greater understanding of the following concepts:

- The European Union and its political and economic goals
- The main institutions of the EU and their organisation and functions
- The symbols of the EU
- The single market and the Eurozone

Competences

This unit covers the following competences:

- Linguistic competence
- Digital competence
- Learning to learn
- Cultural awareness and expression
- Initiative and entrepreneurship
- Social and civic competences

Key Vocabulary

The EU: advantage, citizens, democracy, diversity, equality, flag, freedom, justice, language, motto, partnership, peace, resources, symbolise, united

Institutions: Council of the EU, Court of Auditors, Court of Justice, European Central Bank, European Commission, European Council, European Parliament

People: commissioner, judge, MEP, minister

Eurozone: currency, free, goods, movement, security features, single market, visa

Cambridge English Qualifications practice

You will find **B1 Preliminary for Schools** activity types in the following exercises:
Pupil's Book, Page 76, Activity 3 – Listening Part 3
Activity Book, Page 35, Activity 7– Reading Part 1

Throughout this unit, you will find the following **B1 Preliminary for Schools** vocabulary:
advantage, currency, currently, customer, flag, join, judge, language, nowadays, promote, security, share, together, visa

Materials needed for *Find out more*

- paper
- ruler
- pencil
- scissors
- magnifying glass
- euro notes
- photocopied euro notes

Materials needed for other activities

- paper

Explore

The *Explore* project encourages pupils to write a letter to an EU official. They will research past laws and policies the EU has created, think about a problem, develop a solution and find someone to contact. The different *Explore* stages practise the following skills:

- researching laws and their effects
- analysing a problem
- developing creative solutions
- autonomous investigation and research
- writing a formal persuasive letter

Digital Lab 6 Social Science

Interactive activities

Flashcards

Song: *Different but the same*

Video documentary: *A trip around the EU*

Objective

Pupils will explore the diversity of the European Union by looking at all its official languages and thinking about its motto.

Key vocabulary

advantage, diversity, motto, united

Warm up

- Write the words *united* and *diversity* on the board and elicit definitions from pupils.

- Now, write the motto *United in Diversity* on the board. In small groups, have pupils discuss what it means to them.

Main concepts

- Write two columns on the board: *Countries* and *Languages*. Have pupils complete the table with a European country and its official language(s). Austria – German; Belgium – French, Dutch, German; Bulgaria – Bulgarian; Croatia – Croatian; Cyprus – Greek; Czech Republic – Czech; Denmark – Danish; Estonia – Estonian; Finland – Finnish; France – French; Germany – German; Greece – Greek; Hungary – Hungarian; Ireland – Irish; Italy – Italian; Latvia – Latvian; Lithuania – Lithuanian; Luxembourg – French, German; Malta – Maltese, English; Netherlands – Dutch; Poland –

Pupils' own answers

How is all this diversity an advantage?
Does it cause any difficulties?

S ng
Different but the same

Förenade i mångfalden ❹

Uniţi în diversitate

In Vielfalt geeint ❺

diversity

Združena v raznolikosti

Zjednoczona w różnorodności ❻

D ▶ CUMENTARY
A trip around the EU

Research and write a proposal for the EU. You will:
- investigate what the EU has done to improve our lives.
- think about a problem facing citizens of the EU and develop a solution.
- look up a person to contact in one of the EU institutions.
- write a letter proposing the solution.

69

Polish; Portugal – Portuguese; Romania – Romanian; Slovakia – Slovak; Slovenia – Slovenian; Spain – Spanish; Sweden – Swedish

Learn more

- Tell pupils that the documentary is going to highlight the advantages of being a citizen of the EU and starting a business. Have them brainstorm some ideas before watching and then check if any of their ideas were shown in the video.

Song
This song focuses on the positive factors of the EU. It can be used on pages 70–71

Documentary
The documentary takes pupils on a tour of different countries in the EU. It can be used on pages 68–69 and 70–71.

Tip

There are excellent resources for pupils and teachers on the EU official websites. Encourage pupils to use them and look through them yourself.

Get pupils excited about the project by explaining that they will be making real letters and they will be sent. Tell pupils that this project is about getting involved and taking control of their futures. Real change can come from this project!

Objective

Pupils will learn about the European Union, its symbols, goals, and history.

Key vocabulary

citizens, democracy, equality, flag, freedom, justice, partnership, peace, resources, symbolise

Warm up

- Write the following numbers on the board and have pupils quickly look over the pages and see if they can think of the question that each number answers: *27* (How many countries are in the EU?); *12* (How many stars are on the EU flag?); *6* (How many countries started the EU?); *2002* (When did the euro become the currency of the EU?); *1957* (When did the EU begin?)

Main concepts

- Give pupils time to write five questions where the answers can be found on the page. Then, with books closed, pupils ask a partner their question and try to answer their partner's. Have pupils work with three or four partners. Are there any questions no one could answer?

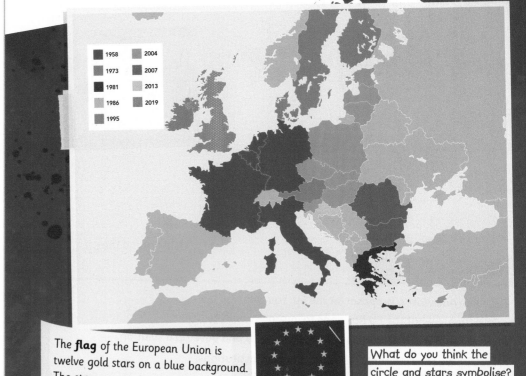

It is a partnership between 27 democratic countries covering most of the European continent that shares power, resources and ideas to create a better life for all its citizens.

WHAT IS THE EU?

Discover... the countries of the EU and its goals.

The **European Union** is a **partnership** between 27 democratic countries covering most of the European continent. The countries share power, resources and ideas to create a better life for all their citizens.

The goals of the EU are:

- To promote peace, democracy and unity.
- To ensure freedom, justice and equality.
- To create a strong and fair economy based on a single market and the euro.
- To promote scientific and technological advancements.
- To protect the environment for future generations.

1958	2004
1973	2007
1981	2013
1986	2019
1995	

The **flag** of the European Union is twelve gold stars on a blue background. The stars are set in a circle.

70

What do you think the circle and stars symbolise?

The circle and stars represent unity, solidarity and harmony. They don't represent the number of countries.

Beethoven

On this day in 1950 the idea of the EU was proposed.

Extra Activity, page 95:

Pupils create a collage about the EU and what it means to them.

Learn more

Listen to the song, *Different but the same*. Tell pupils the tune is from a famous song and ask them if they recognise the tune. Elicit *Ode to Joy* and tell them it is the anthem of the EU and that it hasn't got any words. In groups, have pupils add lyrics to the anthem to sing about the EU in the same way the song did.

Tip

Play *In or out!* In groups, one pupil says a year and a country; the rest of the group has to shout *In* if it was a part of the EU at that time, or *Out* if it wasn't.

After the devastation of the First and Second World Wars, a few countries decided that the best way to prevent this happening again was to work together to control the production of materials needed for war.

Timeline of the EU

1957 The European Union starts with six members

1973 Denmark, Ireland and the United Kingdom join

1981 Greece joins

1986 Spain and Portugal join

Europe Day is celebrated on 9 May. Why did they choose this day?

1995 Austria, Finland and Sweden join

The anthem of the EU is a very famous song. Do you know who wrote it?

2002 The euro becomes the currency of the EU

2004 10 more countries join

2007 Bulgaria and Romania join

What is Brexit? Find out more.

Find another euro hidden in the unit!

2013 Croatia joins, making it 28 countries strong

2019 The United Kingdom leaves the EU?

Explore STAGE 1

- The EU has created many laws and policies to achieve its goals. Research some actions the EU has taken to protect the environment, promote peace and equality and improve the lives of young people.
- Write them down in a chart titled *What the EU has done*.

71

Pupils do their research at home. Help their search results by telling them they should search news stories. Have them share their findings in the next lesson.

Brexit refers to when the citizens of the UK voted to leave the EU. Trying to leave was a very complicated process and took years to accomplish.

Euro on page 72

Objective

Pupils will learn about the institutions of the EU and how decisions are made.

Key vocabulary

commissioner, Council of the EU, Court of Justice, Court of Auditors, European Commission, European Council, European Central Bank, European Parliament, MEP, minister

Warm up

- Write *planner*, *decision-makers* and *regulators* on the board. As a class, think of actions that each group would do. For example; *vote*, *monitor*, *propose*.

Main concepts

- Draw a stick figure on the board with a thought bubble and an idea. Explain that *Mr. Stick* has a great idea for all EU citizens. How can this idea become a law? Pupils copy *Mr Stick* into their notebooks and draw out the steps to become a law as the idea travels through the European Commission to the Parliament and the Council using symbols and arrows.

They do it democratically through the institutions of the EU.

European Commission: Brussels
European Council: Brussels
European Parliament: Strasbourg, Brussels and Luxembourg

HOW DO SO MANY COUNTRIES MAKE DECISIONS TOGETHER?

Discover... the main institutions of the EU.

Just like its member countries, the EU has also got institutions to pass laws and make decisions.

The planners

European Council: Leaders of each country who meet to plan the goals and direction of the EU.

European Commission: A president and 26 commissioners propose laws to the Parliament and the Council of the EU.

European Commission

Do you know who is currently the President of the European Commission?

The decision-makers

European Parliament:

The voice of the people. Its members are called Members of the European Parliament or MEPs.

Together they approve, change or deny proposals from the European Commission. When they approve a proposal, it becomes law.

72

Pupils should look it up online!

Here's the hidden object!

Council of the EU: Brussels
Court of Justice: Luxembourg
Court of Auditors: Luxembourg
European Central Bank: Frankfurt

The European Parliament and Council of the EU are like the Legislative branch. The European Commission and European Council are like the Executive branch.

The regulators

Court of Justice of the EU: One judge from each country. Together they settle disputes between member states and make sure laws are followed and are fair.

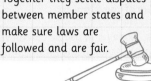

Council of the EU:

Council of the European Union

The voice of the governments. Its members are ministers from each country's government.

European Court of Auditors: Monitors that money is spent and collected properly.

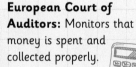

CURIA RATIONUM

European Central Bank: Maintains the stability of the euro.

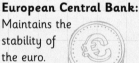

Find out where each institution is located.

Look back

Which institutions seem like the Legislative branch in Spain? Which seem like the Executive?

Explore — STAGE 2

- Though much has been done, there is still work to do. Make a list of some problems the EU or the world still faces. It could be the environment, creating jobs or helping those in need.
- Choose an area you want to help and look up a person or organisation to contact. Write down their name, position, contact address and email address.

73

Have pupils brainstorm in small groups and guide them if they are having trouble thinking of tangible ideas. Once pupils choose an area to help, ask: *Who can we contact?* Direct pupils to the official EU websites. Tell them that if they don't find the right person to contact, their great idea will never be heard. Check their findings in the next lesson.

Objective

Pupils will learn what the single market and Eurozone are and how they affect our lives.

Key vocabulary

currency, Eurozone, free, goods, movement, single market, visa

Warm up

- Write *19* on the board and ask the pupils what they think it represents. Elicit: *The number of countries in the Eurozone*. See how many can be named as a class.

Main concepts

- First, pupils act out one of the cartoons and add some more dialogue to the script. Then, they take the same scene, but act it out as if it were happening today showing the advantages of the single market. Allow them time to practise and even create new situations not shown in the book.

Learn more

- Play *In the Zone*. In groups, one pupil names a country. The other pupils make a letter with their body to answer: *Z* if it is in the Eurozone, a *U* if it is only in the EU or an *O* if it is out of the EU. One point is awarded to the first pupil to get the correct answer.

Poland: Zloty	Croatia: Kuna
Sweden: Krona	Romania: Leu
Czech Republic: Koruna	Bulgaria: Lev
Hungary: Forint	Denmark: Krone

If you are in the Eurozone, yes!

The Eurozone

CAN I SPEND MY EUROS HERE?

The creation of the euro and the single market is one of the greatest achievements of the EU.

In a single market, goods, money and people can move freely from one country to another. Why is this an advantage?

Discover... how the single market and the euro affect your daily life.

What do we call the group of countries that uses the euro?

Life before the EU

Sorry. If you want to work here, you'll have to apply for a visa.

I would sell these all over Europe if it wasn't so difficult and expensive.

I wish there were more products from other countries; there just aren't enough options.

Nowadays, it is easier and cheaper to buy from other EU countries. Businesses can have customers all over the EU. That means more options for you and more customers for businesses. The free movement of people allows citizens to work and study in any country.

Look back...

What year did Spain change to the euro?

Which EU countries don't use the euro?

What currency do they use?

Explore STAGE 3

- Find other pupils who chose the same area as you and brainstorm ideas.
- Create a plan for a law to help with your problems. Share the people and organisations you found in Stage 2 and decide who to contact.

74

I think we should contact ...

Let's write to ...

In 2002

Group pupils according to the area they want to help. Give pupils time to discuss ideas in their group. Tell them that together they need to form a law or proposal. It doesn't have to be too detailed but at least an action and its effect. Pupils share the officials they found and decide who to contact. It can be multiple people.

For next lesson ... paper, ruler, pencil, scissors, magnifying glass, euro notes, photocopied euro notes

HOW IS MONEY MADE?

Find Out more...

Discover... the features of the euro notes.

Background: Imagine the EU wants to make a 19 euro note to celebrate the Eurozone and has asked your class to help design its front side. Their requirements are:

- It must be bigger than a 10 euro note but smaller than a 20 euro note.
- It must have security features.
- It must reflect the EU motto *United in diversity*.

Materials: paper, ruler, pencil, scissors, magnifying glass, 10 or 20 euro notes

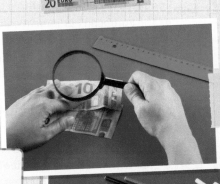

Task: Design a new 19 euro note.

- Measure the height and length of the 10 and 20 euro notes and record them in your notebook.
- Explore the security features. Hold a note up to the light, tilt the note forward and backward under a light and use a magnifying glass to examine the note closely. Record your observations in your notebook.
- Brainstorm ideas for images or a design you could use to represent the EU and its motto.
- Decide the size and layout of your note. Where will the numbers and images go?
- Decide on the security features you will include.
- Draw and colour. Make sure to record where the hidden security features are.

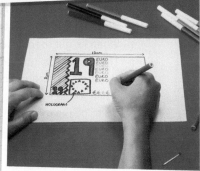

When I ... , I can see ...

There is a change when I ...

75

Objective

Pupils will find out more about the features of euro notes and design their own.

Key language

hologram, ink, security features, watermark

Warm up

- Show pupils a real and a fake photocopied euro note. Ask: *Which one is real? How do you know?* Then, have pupils close their eyes and feel the notes. Can they feel which is fake? How?

Main concepts

- Give each group one euro note at a time and keep track of the bills by writing down what each group takes and when it returns.

- When pupils are exploring the security features, write some vocabulary on the board and explain it to help them better describe the notes: *ink, reflective, shiny, hologram, watermark, translucent, transparent*

Learn more

- Have pupils give a quick presentation of their new note. They must describe how it fits the motto of the EU and explain its security features.

Language Review
answers

1 1 e

2 c

3 a

4 d

5 b

2 a itself

b myself

c themselves

d yourself

e herself

3 a a blog

b size

c 705

d MEPs

e art

f artist

This activity gives pupils practice of *B1 Preliminary for Schools* Listening Part 3.

Language Review

1 **In your notebook, match the sentence halves using the first and second conditional.**

1 If that country were in the EU, …
2 You will have to exchange your money …
3 If you want to work in another EU country, …
4 If I went to a hospital in Germany, …
5 The proposal will become law …

a … you don't have to apply for a visa.
b … if Parliament approves it.
c … if you leave the Eurozone.
d … I wouldn't have to pay any extra money.
e … I would study there.

2 **Complete the sentences with a reflexive pronoun.**

a The European Parliament can't approve laws by ….. . It needs the approval of the Council of the EU as well.
b I didn't go on holiday with my friends or family. I travelled through Europe by ….. .
c The townspeople couldn't build the community centre ….. , so they applied for help from the EU.
d You can decide ….. on which MEP to vote for.
e She was feeling very sorry for ….. because she had lost the election.

3  **You will hear David describe his trip to Brussels. Complete the sentences using one or two words, a number, a date or a time.**

a Before leaving on his trip, David read ….. about the European Parliament.
b When he got there he couldn't believe the ….. of the Parliament.
c The Hemicycle can seat all ….. Members of Parliament.
d David found the names of the ….. to be the most difficult things to say correctly.
e He enjoyed the ….. the most.
f He would like to be an ….. in the future.

Encourage pupils to revise the unit content using the techniques on page 89.

Content Review answers

1 a European Parliament, MEPs; Council of the EU, ministers

b European Council, leaders of each country; European Commission, commissioners; Court of Justice, judges

c European Commission, commissioners

d European Council, leaders of each country

e European Parliament, MEPs

f European Central Bank

2 Goals of the EU promote peace, ensure freedom and democracy, create a strong and fair single market, promote scientific and technological advancements, protect the environment

Elements of the European Single Market; free movement of goods, free movement of people, free movement of money

---

Content Review

1 Read the clues and write the institution(s) and their members.

a Approves laws.
b Contains only one member from each country.
c Proposes laws.
d Decides the goals of the EU.
e Represents the citizens.
f Regulates the euro.

Assessment link
For more Unit 6 activities go to page 88.

2 Copy and complete the diagrams.

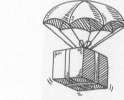

promote peace

goals of the EU

free movement of goods

elements of the European Single Market

Explore — FINALE

- Now it's time to make your voice heard! With your group, plan out how to organise your letter. Is it formal or informal? Who are you writing to? What is the goal of your law? How will it work?

- Write your letter and send it to the person or organisation you chose. Be sure to give them an address to reply!

Dear Sir / Madam, ...

We are writing to you to ...

77

Planning the structure of the letter should be done as a class. Instruct pupils on proper openings and formal language that must be used. Then, pupils can discuss what they should say and how to say it. Remind the group that everyone will be writing a letter, so they should all take notes. Have pupils write the letter at home. You can scan or copy them to email or send out the best ones by mail and have pupils in the same group sign the bottom.

Think about it answers

1 To prevent another world war by sharing important resources.

2 To promote peace, ensure freedom and democracy, create a strong and fair single market, promote scientific and technological advancements and protect the environment.

3 There are 27 countries in the EU and 19 in the Eurozone.

4 The flag is a blue background with a circle of 12 gold stars. Europe Day is 9 May. It marks the day the EU was first proposed in 1950. It's a celebration of peace, harmony and diversity. Its motto is *United in Diversity* and represents the values of the EU.

5 First, the European Commission meets, creates a plan and proposes the law to the European Parliament and the Council of the EU. They separately debate and vote. If both houses approve it, it becomes law.

6 A group made up of leaders from each country that meet to set the goals and direction of the EU.

7 Members of the European Parliament or MEPs are voted into the Parliament by the citizens of their countries.

8 The European Central Bank and the European Court of Auditors.

9 A single market is an area of multiple countries where money, people and goods can move freely across borders.

10 Consumers have more choice of products. Phone plans and airfares are cheaper. Students have many more options of places to study. Small businesses have access to many more customers.

Think harder answers

1 Example answers: There could have been more wars. There would have been less diversity. Fewer scientific advancements. More difficult to travel, study and work in different European countries.

2 The EU set a goal to have 20% of energy from renewable sources by 2020. The EU creates protected areas for wildlife and sea life. It sets limits of how much pollution cars and factories can emit.

3 Pupils' own answers

4 Pupils' own answers

5 It is an area of almost all EU countries where people can travel freely without border checks.

6 Customers have more choices and competition creates lower prices. Businesses have access to millions more customers and employees.

7 Example answers: They are very similar in the division of powers and the three branches, Executive, Legislative and Judicial. They are different in that the MEPs are voted directly into the Parliament and in Spain the people vote for the party. The head of the Executive branch and roles of ministers are rotated, but in Spain each person is chosen specifically for each role.

8 Pupils' own answers

9 Pupils' own answers

10 Pupils' own answers

UNIT 6 TRACKLIST

Track 35   page 69, Song *Different but the same*

Track 36   page 70, *What is the EU?*

Track 37   page 72, *How do so many countries make decisions together?*

Track 38   page 74, *Can I spend my euros here?*

Track 39   page 76, Language Review, Listening activity 3

AUDIO SCRIPT

WELCOME UNIT

Track 02 Page 5, Listening Activity (*B1 Preliminary for Schools Listening Part 1*)

Listen to pupils talk about different jobs. Which photos are they describing?

Pupil 1: I think this job would be best for me. I love investigating about the past. I also love history and exploring other cultures.

Pupil 2: This job looks interesting. I'm really good at reading maps, but I like cities much more than nature. Look at those designs! It would be amazing to build something like that.

Pupil 3: That job looks exciting. There are so many important events happening in the world and she is right in the middle of it. I definitely need a job where I can be at events like this one. Plus, I love being in front of the camera.

UNIT 1

Track 03 Page 7, Song *Autonomous communities*

(Chorus)
Spain has seventeen of these
What are they called?
Can you tell me, if you please?
Autonomous communities!

Castilla y León has the biggest area
Galicia the Atlantic coast
Cantabria by the Mar Cantábrico
Aragón, where the Ebro flows

Canarias has a subtropical climate
Asturias is a principality

Comunidad Valenciana
Is by the Mediterranean Sea
(Chorus)
Islas Baleares have many islands
La Rioja has the smallest population
Murcia has only one province
Andalucía has the largest population

Cataluña shares a border with France
Extremadura is next to Portugal
País Vasco also borders France
Navarra is a Comunidad Foral
(Chorus)
Castilla-La Mancha has five provinces
Comunidad de Madrid has only one
But it is the capital of Spain
And has the third highest population
(Chorus)

Track 06 Page 10, Listening Activity (*B1 Preliminary for Schools Listening Part 3*)

Listen to two friends planning a trip. Write down the places and activities they mention.

Girl: We've got to start planning our summer holiday. How would you like to visit Toledo? There are so many museums to visit there.

Boy: My aunt lives near the Tajo, so I've been many times. I'd prefer to go somewhere else, maybe the Sistema Ibérico? Did you know it passes through five communities?

Girl: Hmmm, I've already been hiking there with my family. What about Santander in Cantabria?

Boy: What a good idea! On the way we can stop in the Picos de Europa to go mountain biking. They border the northern edge of the Meseta.

Girl: Great! I've always wanted to visit the Cordillera Cantábrica. We can go kayaking on the Sella.

Boy: And when we get there, we can go surfing in the Mar Cantábrico!

Girl: This is going to be an awesome trip!

UNIT 2

Track 09   Page 19, Song *Cruising the continent*

Let's go east

And check out Russia

Home to a river

We call the Volga

Let's go west

To the Republic of Ireland

The "Emerald Isle"

Is what we call this island

(Chorus)

Cruising the continent

Couldn't be more content

Travelling in Europe

I never wanna give it up!

Let's go south

To lovely Portugal

The mouth of the Tajo

Is in Lisbon, its capital

(Chorus)

Let's go north

To cold Finland

To see reindeer

In beautiful Lapland

(Chorus)

Track 11   Page 20, Listening Activity (*B1 Preliminary for Schools Listening Part 3*)

Listen to the weather report for capital cities in Europe. Write down the cities you hear and match them to their countries.

Meteorologist: Hello and good evening, here's your weekend weather forecast across the continent. In the north, temperatures will be below freezing with strong winds on the Scandinavian Peninsula, so watch out everyone in Oslo and Stockholm. In central Europe expect stormy conditions with snowfall in the Alps around Bern, and as the storm heads east, showers and lightning in Prague and Vienna. Down south on the Balkan Peninsula, it will be dry and warm. Expect lots of sunshine in Sofia and Bucharest, but there will be more clouds near Athens.

UNIT 3

Track 14   Page 29, Song *Dos de Mayo*

No king in Madrid, he was in France

The people grew worried as French soldiers advanced

In front of the Palace, Madrileños were found

Stopping French soldiers from entering the grounds

(Chorus)

The 2ⁿᵈ of May, eighteen hundred and eight

Here in Spain, we remember that date

The people rose up, united as one

Against the troops of Napoleon

The fighting began, spread all through the streets

But at the end of the day, it was a Spanish defeat

On the 2ⁿᵈ of May, the battle was lost

We'll never forget those whose lives it cost

(Chorus)

Track 20 Page 40, Listening Activity (*B1 Preliminary for Schools Listening Part 4*)

You will hear Pamela talking about her visit to the Prado Museum. For each question choose the correct answer.

Pamela: I finally made it to the Prado. I was going to go last year with my grandmother on my birthday, but we couldn't. Luckily, we are studying the Modern Age in class and my teacher planned an excursion to see the art from that time period. On the bus ride, I was excited about seeing all the art. When the bus arrived, there were so many people. There were some school groups like us but also large tourist groups from all over the world who come to Madrid to visit the museum. When I first entered the museum, I couldn't believe its size! There were so many rooms and so much art. It felt like you would have to run to see everything, but you couldn't do that because you would break something. Our guide showed us all of Francisco de Goya's paintings. We started with his early works; when he mainly painted colour and happy scenes of daily life. Next, we went and saw his most famous works, like *Dos de Mayo*. I enjoyed seeing those because I recognised them from our books in school and it was cool to see them in real life. I still liked his earlier paintings better, they made me smile. Especially the one of a woman in the park with an umbrella, called *El Parasol*. We ended the tour looking at Goya's Black Paintings. He painted these later in his life and you could call them … well … interesting. They were scenes painted in dark colours with scary images. Some of my classmates felt sad looking at them but I was just frightened. I loved the Prado and will definitely return, but I want to see more art first. So, next I will visit the *Reina Sofía* and maybe even take art classes this summer!

UNIT 4

Track 21 Page 43 Song, *All these new things*

(Chorus)
Lots of new technology
Modernising society
The world is changing so quickly
All these new things for you and me

I moved to the city
Got a job in a factory
Now I work with big machines
That get their power from steam

(Chorus)

The owner of the factory
Is a member of the bourgeoisie
Who joined nobility
Because they made lots of money

(Chorus)

I'm in the middle class
My small business is growing fast
New inventions, like the train
Let me sell products all over Spain

(Chorus)

Track 24 Page 46, Listening Activity (*B1 Preliminary for Schools Listening Part 3*)

Listen to a report on the Industrial Revolution in Spain. Write down the places you hear and what they produced.

Narrator: The Industrial Revolution began in the United Kingdom around 1833, one hundred years before it arrived in Spain. It was brought on by new forms of energy like steam and inventions that could produce things faster with less work done by humans. In Spain, the process was slow, and Cataluña was the only area to be industrialised by the early 19th century. Machines like the Spinning Jenny and its new railway made Cataluña the biggest producer of textiles in the Mediterranean. In the North, País Vasco and Cantabria mined materials to make iron and steel. The steam engine was powered by coal and Asturias began to produce more and more coal to meet the needs of Europe. Unfortunately, the lack of a railway network, political instability and wars stopped Spain from completely industrialising until the late 20th century.

UNIT 5

Track 29 Page 57 Song *It's my right!*

(Chorus)

Hey hey, I'm here to say
I learned all about the Constitution today
I learned my rights, as you will see
Why don't you put some questions to me?

Alright, alright. What about …
… expressing how you feel?
It's my right!
… seeing the doctor when you're ill?
It's my right!
… freedom of religion?
Yes, it's my right!
… a brand-new television?
That's not my right!

(Chorus)

OK, OK. What about …
… a school and a teacher?
It's my right!
… choosing a leader?
It's my right!
… live in any part of Spain?
Yes, it's my right!
… learning to fly a plane?
That's not my right!

(Chorus)

OK, alright. What about …
… taking part in a protest?
It's my right!
… a home that's decent?
It's my right!
… going on strike?
Yes, it's my right!
… and dropping the mic?
It's not my right. But I think I'll do it!

Track 33 Page 63, Listening Activity (*B1 Preliminary for Schools Listening Part 3*)

Listen to a woman talking to a group of pupils about her job as a deputy in Congress. Write down three things she has to do today.

Deputy: Hello kids, how are you today? Welcome to the *Congreso de Diputados*. Here we are on the front steps between these two famous lions. Does anyone know their names? They are named after two heroes from the uprising on 2 May 1808.

Pupil: *Daoíz* and *Valverde*?

Deputy: Yes, excellent job. OK, let's go! Here is the *Salon de Sesiones*. This is where we vote, debate and discuss any laws or proposals. In fact, later today we are voting on an important proposal. I even have to stand right there and tell the entire Congress about why they should vote for the proposal. Would you like to see my office? Let's go.

Here is where I do most of my work, researching laws, studying their effects and communicating with the people. I answer lots of emails and letters from concerned citizens. It is important that I hear what the people think, after all we are their voice in the government. Before you came, I was reading a letter from a group of students that are concerned about pollution in their neighbourhood. I am going to have a meeting with them this afternoon.

[phone rings] Sorry boys and girls, I have to answer this. Why doesn't everyone head to the library of congress and take some pictures and I'll meet up with you later.

UNIT 6

Track 35   Page 69, Song *Different but the same*

We are different but the same
All of us European
Our differences make us stronger
Build ties over land and water
Promote peace, democracy
Protect freedom and equality
Twenty-seven work as one
It's the European Union

(Repeat all)

Track 39   Page 76, Listening Activity (*B1 Preliminary for Schools Listening Part 1*)

You will hear David describe his trip to Brussels. Complete the sentences using one or two words, a number, a date or a time.

David: When my family announced that we were visiting Belgium on holiday, I wasn't very excited. So, I decided to do some research and find out what there was to do there. I was surprised to learn you can visit the European Parliament when I read a blog about a student's experience there. She made it sound like it was a must-see when in Belgium. On the second day, I convinced my family to take the bus with me and see the parliament. As we got to the stop I looked out of the window and couldn't believe the size of it. It was much bigger than I thought. This made sense when the guide explained that it has to seat all 705 Members of Parliament at the same time. When we were in the Hemicycle, where the MEPs debate and vote, I walked around looking for where the Spanish representatives sat. My sister and I tried to read some of the names and with so many MEPs from all 27 countries of the EU we didn't know how to pronounce many of them. After that, the guide let us explore the *Parlamentarium*. It's an interactive visitors centre explaining the history and function of the EU. There was also an art exhibit by young artists from the EU. I loved this because I would like to be an artist in the future.

ACTIVITY BOOK ANSWERS

UNIT 1

1

	Land boundary	Water boundary
To the north	France, Andorra	Mar Cantábrico
To the east	----	Mediterranean Sea
To the south	Morocco, Gibraltar	Mediterranean Sea, Atlantic Ocean
To the west	Portugal	Atlantic Ocean

2

t	i	g	x	g	a	k	g	a	s	t	u
l	o	g	r	o	ñ	o	n	o	z	u	b
t	y	j	k	a	y	o	y	w	b	f	z
a	v	t	l	j	l	a	i	s	o	s	s
e	u	w	o	e	d	g	a	v	a	v	e
m	u	r	c	i	a	z	j	m	n	i	v
x	p	r	r	s	o	m	c	u	t	e	i
j	a	é	y	g	f	g	q	f	a	d	l
b	m	h	a	s	k	d	o	x	n	o	l
i	g	r	f	z	f	m	b	t	d	i	a
p	a	m	p	l	o	n	a	s	e	b	k
z	r	m	a	d	r	i	d	m	r	t	a

3

Pupil's own answers

4

b Montes de Toledo

c Tajo

d Sistema Ibérico

e Cordillera Cantábrica

f Montes de León

g Sistema Central

h Miño

i Sierra Morena

j Guadalquivir

k Guadiana

5

1 e

2 f

3 c

4 b

5 k

6 i

7 h

8 a

9 d

10 g

11 j

6

b false

c true

d false

e false

7

2 a

3 e

4 b

8

Islas Canarias: *seven main islands, formed by volcanos*

Islas Baleares: five main islands, sit in the Mediterranean Sea

Both: have no permanent rivers

9

2 b

3 a

4 c

10

Pupils' own answers

11

b Pyrenees

c Ter

d Cordillera Costero-Catalana

e Llobregat

f Segura

g Sistemas Béticos

h Júcar

i Ebro

j Nalón

k Macizo Galaico

12

Pupil's own answers

ACTIVITY BOOK ANSWERS

1

a Arctic Ocean

b Black Sea

c Atlantic Ocean

d Mediterranean Sea

e Caspian Sea

2

a Spain   **d** Russia

b Macedonia   **e** Germany

c France

3

(Crossword 1)

Across

2 Rome   7 Ljubljana

4 Helsinki   8 Brussels

Down

1 Zagreb   5 Ireland

2 Russia   6 Bulgaria

3 Minsk

(Crossword 2)

Across

3 Bern   7 Reykjavik

6 Latvia

Down

1 Budapest   4 Oslo

2 Germany   5 Ankara

4

Name	Length	Watershed	Interesting Information
Rhine	*1,233 km*	*Atlantic*	Starts in the Alps
Volga	3,500 km	*Caspian*	*The longest river in Europe*
Seine	*776 km*	Atlantic	*Passes under 37 bridges in Paris*
Thames	*346 km*	Atlantic	It has over 80 islands
Danube	2,856 km	Black Sea	*Runs through ten countries*

5

(Pupils produce a graph with the following information)

Volga: 3,500 km; Rhine: 1,233 km; Danube: 2,856 km; Thames: 346 km; Seine: 776 km

6

a <u>Alps;</u> The Caucasus Mountains contain the highest peak in Europe.

b <u>north;</u> Most of the mountain ranges are found in the south of Europe.

c <u>Elbrus;</u> Mount Etna is Europe's most active volcano.

d <u>Russia;</u> The Ural Mountains form the eastern border of Europe.

e <u>Alps;</u> The Danube River runs between the Carpathian and the Balkan Mountains.

7

a The Alps

b The Pyrenees

c Caucasus Mountains

d Sistemas Béticos

e The Alps

8

a Red Sea; The Red Sea does not form a border of the European continent.

b The Netherlands; The Netherlands is not an island.

c Volga; The Volga drains into the Caspian Sea, while the other rivers drain into the Black Sea.

d Ural Mountains; The Ural Mountains are in the northeast of Europe while the other mountains are in the south.

9

a 2   **h** 1

b 4   **i** 8

c 13   **j** 3

d 5   **k** 10

e 12   **l** 9

f 11   **m** 6

g 7

10

a France, Italy, Switzerland, Germany, Austria, Slovenia

b Russia, Georgia, Azerbaijan

c Italy

d Germany, Austria, Slovakia, Hungary, Croatia, Serbia, Bulgaria, Romania, Moldova, Ukraine

e Czech Republic, Germany

11

1 b   **2** d   **3** c

UNIT 3

1

a A system of government where the monarch has all the power.

b A system of government where the monarch's power is limited by a constitution.

c A political belief centred around individual freedoms and social progress.

d Usually a violent event by the people to change their leader.

2

Example answer: The French Revolution began with an uprising from the peasant class. It succeeded, and the absolute monarchy was changed to a constitutional monarchy. The new government was having problems and kings from all around Europe did not like the new liberalism and declared war on France. General Napoleon Bonaparte defended France and when he returned to Paris declared himself ruler and ended the revolution.

3

a Napoleon

b Carlos IV

c The people of Madrid

d Manuel Godoy

e Joseph Bonaparte

f Napoleon

4

a Carlos IV appointed Manuel Godoy as his royal advisor.

b Manual Godoy signed a treaty with France to conquer Portugal.

c Napoleon invaded Spain.

d Napoleon forced Carlos IV and Fernando VII to leave Spain and Joseph Bonaparte was named King of Spain by his brother.

e the people of Madrid rose up against the French soldiers in their city.

5

Pupils' own answers. Make sure pupils have a proper greeting and closing of an email. When making a suggestion they could use, *How/What about … You could/should … .* Pupils must respond or comment on all three notes.

6

a false   **c** false   **e** true

b true   **d** true   **f** true

7

a Traditionalism   **d** Traditionalism

b Liberalism   **e** Liberalism

c Liberalism

8

a Paraguay   **e** Ecuador

b Argentina   **f** Bolivia, Uruguay

c Chile

d Venezuela, Colombia,

9

Fernando VII: The Constitution of 1812 was revoked; A brief period called the Liberal Triennium; Many of Spain's American territories were lost.
María Cristina: The Carlist party was formed; The Carlist Wars; A constitutional monarchy ruled
Isabel II: The Carlist Wars; A revolution took place in 1868

10

a An Italian brought to Spain to be king. He was king from 1871–1873.

b In 1873.   **c** 11 months.

11

a taught   **b** more   **c** job

d them   **e** given

12

Pupils' own answers. Check for use of vocabulary; *brighter, happier, darker, pessimistic*. Painting A was painted early in Goya's career and B in his later career.

13

Cause	Effect
The French Republic brought new ideas.	…
…	The War of Independence started.
The Constitution of 1812 was written.	…
…	The Constitution was declared illegal.
…	Carlist Wars began.

14

Left his *valido* to do most of the work; Fernando VII; Joseph Bonaparte; Revoked the Constitution of 1812; María Cristina; Isabel II; supported liberal ideas; He was not very popular and stepped down.

ACTIVITY BOOK ANSWERS

1

Alfonso XII: Ruled during a time of stability; Died while in power

Alfonso XIII: Became king at birth; Supported the dictator Miguel Primo de Rivera

Both: Used the *turno pacífico*

2

1 b   **2** e   **3** a   **4** c   **5** d

3

a true   **c** false

b true   **d** false

4

a upper class (nobility and bourgeoisie)

b middle class

c working class

5

a bourgeoisie   **d** middle class

b working class   **e** upper class

c nobility   **f** working class

6

a Republicans

b Both

c Nationalists

d Republicans

e Nationalists

f Nationalists

g Republicans

7

Pupils' own answers. Pupils should know that in photo A society is modernising, more people are moving to the cities and new technologies are changing the world. They should note in photo B that all the progress of photo A has been lost. Life is very difficult. They could mention people imprisoned, food shortages, etc.

8

a Autarky is when a country tries to be self-sufficient.

b Food shortages caused rationing of essential items.

c Some people who opposed Franco were imprisoned or killed.

d Unions and political parties were illegal.

e The press, films and books were censored.

f Life during these times was difficult for many.

9

The Restoration: 1875, 1931; Constitutional Monarchy; time of stability and modernisation

The Second Republic: 1931, 1939; Republic; a lot of progress and social reforms, but also of unrest and civil war

Franco's dictatorship: 1939, 1975; Dictatorship; some of the population suffered from the economic crisis and restricted civil liberties

10

a 3   **b** 1   **c** 5   **d** 4   **e** 2

11

Example answers: Spain joined NATO in 1982. In 1986, Spain entered the European Union. Spain replaced the peseta with the euro in 2002.

12

a since   **d** for

b who   **e** This

c any   **f** with

13

a María Cristina

b Adolfo Suárez

c Alfonso XII

d Francisco Franco

e Alfonso XIII

14

a Spain replaced the peseta with the euro.

b Alfonso XIII was named king.

c Adolfo Suárez was appointed as Prime Minister.

d Spain lost its last overseas territories.

e Spain joined the EU.

15

a 1931   **d** 1939

b 1875   **e** 1936

c 1977   **f** 1923

UNIT 5

1

a Right to compulsory school education.

b Right to strike; freedom of assembly; freedom of expression.

c Right and duty to vote.

2

The people must: take care of the environment, pay taxes, respect the law

The state must: provide health care, give free school education, create opportunities for work

The people have: freedom to travel, voting rights, freedom of speech

3

a Executive

b Legislative

c Executive

d Judicial

e Legislative

4

a To oversee that no one violates the Constitution.

b To represent Spain in foreign affairs.

5

a true

b false

c true

d true

e false

f true

6

2 makes laws

3 Executive

4 Senate

5 Congress

6 Deputies

7 Judges/Magistrates

8 The people

9 Ministers

7

Missing provinces: La Coruña, Orense, Valladolid, Burgos, Salamanca, Álava, Huesca, Girona, Tarragona, Alicante, Cuenca, Ciudad Real, Badajoz, Granada, Sevilla, Las Palmas, Cantabria, La Rioja, León, Huelva

8

a municipality

b province

c municipality

d autonomous community

e autonomous community

9

1 b

2 a

3 c

10

Across

2 right

6 duty

7 equality

8 parliamentary

9 deputies

Down

1 fifty

3 judge

4 legislative

6 constitution

ACTIVITY BOOK ANSWERS

1

a ✓ b ✓ c ✓ d

2

1 b 2 d 3 a 4 c

3

a Croatia 2013

b Netherlands 1957

c Sweden 1995

d Poland 2004

4

a Norway, Iceland, Liechtenstein, Albania, Switzerland, Turkey, Russia, Macedonia, Montenegro, the UK

b Bulgaria, Croatia, Czech Republic, Denmark, Hungary, Poland, Romania, Sweden

c France, Germany, Italy, Netherlands, Belgium, Luxembourg

d Austria, Belgium, Cyprus, Estonia, Finland, France, Germany, Greece, Ireland, Italy, Latvia, Lithuania, Luxembourg, Malta, the Netherlands, Portugal, Slovakia, Slovenia, Spain

5

MEPs, European Parliament, Approve laws

Ministers, Council of the EU, Approve laws

Leaders of each country, European Council, Decide direction and goals of EU

Commissioners, European Commission, Propose new laws

6

a European Commission

b European Parliament

c Council of the EU

d MEPs

e leaders

7

1 a   2 b   3 c   4 a

8

a Free movement of people

b Free movement of goods

c Free movement of money

d If citizens of the EU can't find work in their country, they can look for work in any EU country.

e Businesses have access to all the people in the EU as customers.

f Travellers don't need to change currency if they are staying in the Eurozone.

9

a six countries joined together to create the EU.

b the euro became the official currency of the EU.

c a goal of the EU.

d consists of 19 countries that use the euro as their currency.

e the European Parliament and the Council of the EU have to approve a proposal.

10

a false

b false

c true

d false

e true

11

Pupils' own answers

12

Pupils' own answers